BUSINESS ISSUES, COMPETITION AND ENTREPRENEURSHIP

THE LABOR FORCE PARTICIPATION RATE

DECLINES, IMPLICATIONS AND CAUSES

BUSINESS ISSUES, COMPETITION AND ENTREPRENEURSHIP

Additional books in this series can be found on Nova's website under the Series tab.

Additional e-books in this series can be found on Nova's website under the e-book tab.

BUSINESS ISSUES, COMPETITION AND ENTREPRENEURSHIP

THE LABOR FORCE PARTICIPATION RATE

DECLINES, IMPLICATIONS AND CAUSES

DARREL GRAVES
EDITOR

New York

For permission to use material from this book please contact us:
Telephone 631-231-7269; Fax 631-231-8175
Web Site: http://www.novapublishers.com

Additional color graphics may be available in the e-book version of this book.

Library of Congress Cataloging-in-Publication Data

ISBN: 978-1-63463-391-8

Published by Nova Science Publishers, Inc. † New York

Contents

Preface **vii**

Chapter 1 The Labor Force Participation Rate Since 2007: Causes and Policy Implications **1**
Council of Economic Advisers

Chapter 2 Returning to Full Employment: What Do the Indicators Tell Us? **61**
Marc Labonte

Chapter 3 The Increase in Unemployment Since 2007: Is It Cyclical or Structural? **85**
Linda Levine

Index **109**

PREFACE

This book analyzes the evolution of the labor force participation rate since late 2007 and attempts to quantify the effects of these various forces.

Chapter 1 – In 2008, the U.S. economy collided with two historic forces. The first force was the Great Recession, the most severe economic crisis in a generation. While the economy has recovered considerably over the last five years, there is little doubt that more work remains to address some of the challenges left in the wake of the Great Recession. The turmoil of 2008 inflicted tremendous pain on millions of families, overshadowing the fact that 2008 also marked a unique milestone in U.S. economic history. That year, the first baby boomers (those born in 1946) turned 62 and became eligible for Social Security early retirement benefits. This second force—the demographic inflection point stemming from the retirement of the baby boomers—was felt far less acutely than the Great Recession, but will continue to have a profound influence on the economy for years to come, well after the business cycle recovery from the Great Recession is considered complete.

In addition to these inflection points in 2008, a number of longer-term trends had been playing out in the U.S. labor force prior to 2008—and have continued since then. These include the nearly continuous decline in labor force participation rates for prime-age males (i.e., age 25-54) since the mid-1950s and the dramatic rise in labor force participation rates for prime-age females in the 1970s and 1980s followed by a stalling and slight trend decline after the late 1990s.

Many dimensions of the economy's performance over the last several years can only be properly evaluated when the effects of the Great Recession, the retirement boom, and the longer-term labor force trends are taken into account. One of the clearest illustrations of this point is the labor force participation rate, which represents the fraction of the adult population either working or looking for work. Changes in labor force participation reflect not just current economic conditions like job availability and workers' assessments of job-finding prospects, but also more structural factors like the age distribution of the population and other aspects of society that impact people's decisions to participate in the labor force.

This report analyzes the evolution of the labor force participation rate since late 2007 and attempts to quantify the effects of these various forces. We examine the period since 2007 to focus on how each of the two largest forces, the Great Recession and the retirement of the baby boomers, has impacted labor force participation in recent years. We find that the combination of demographic changes and the drop in labor force participation that would have been expected based on historical business cycle patterns explain most but not all of the recent drop in labor force participation. This implies that other factors, likely including both a continuation of pre- existing trends in labor force participation by certain groups and the unique effects of the Great Recession have also been important. This report also discusses the labor force participation rates for different groups, discusses potential future scenarios for the participation rate, and lays out policies that would help to boost participation in the years to come.

Chapter 2 – Until recently, the economy and labor market were experiencing an unusually slow recovery from the longest and deepest recession since the Great Depression compared to other expansions since World War II. The rapid decline in the unemployment rate from 7.9% in January to 6.7% in December 2013 (where it remained in the first quarter of 2014) would seem to indicate that the labor market is returning to normal. The current unemployment rate is only 0.5 to 1.5 percentage points higher than the consensus range of full employment.

Unusually, the unemployment rate may not currently be a good proxy for the overall state of the labor market or economy. Some of the decline in the unemployment rate in 2013 is attributable to a recovery in employment, but some is attributable to workers dropping out of the labor force. The labor force participation rate has continued to fall during the recovery and is at its lowest level since the 1970s. In fact, it has fallen more in the past five years than at any time since data have been collected. Studies have identified multiple reasons for the decline. Some workers have left the labor force because they have become discouraged and given up on seeking employment. Others have left for reasons stemming from long-term trends that are unrelated to the recession, such as age or enrollment in school or training. This trend could reverse—for example, more workers returned to the labor force than found jobs in the first quarter of 2014, which prevented the unemployment rate from falling. Other evidence also points to more slack in the economy than the headline unemployment rate suggests. Economic output and employment have grown since mid-2009 and 2010, respectively, but at relatively sluggish rates. The long-term unemployment rate and youth unemployment rates have fallen only modestly since the recession ended and are still at historically high levels. Inflation has remained slightly lower than the Federal Reserve's (Fed's) goal of 2%. These other economic indicators could be sending a misleading signal about significant slack in the economy, however, if the economy's potential capacity has been eroded by structural changes or by the length and depth of the Great Recession. Cyclical deterioration in the U.S. labor market is usually considered temporary—recessions are thought to have no lasting effect on overall employment and unemployment rates. This recession could cause a departure from conventional wisdom if labor market problems that started as cyclical persisted so long that they became structural. For example, long-term unemployment could have caused workers' skills to erode, which would then prevent them from finding a job when the economy recovered.

Congress conducts fiscal policy and oversees the Fed's implementation of monetary policy, the two tools of macroeconomic stabilization. Policy makers are grappling with the transition from the highly expansionary monetary and fiscal policy put in place during the Great Recession. Many economists advocate reducing the budget deficit only when the economy is at or near full employment. Likewise, the Fed has stated that it would begin to raise interest rates once the economy is near full employment. If the economy remains far from full employment, then declining unemployment would not yet call for a tightening of monetary and fiscal policy. Alternatively, if lower unemployment is being driven by a cyclical upswing and the economy is now closer to full employment than historical experience would predict, policy would likely need to be tightened sooner in order to avoid rising inflation. It would also suggest that structural policies (e.g., those that increase the incentives to hire, seek work, delay retirement, or train) would be more effective at improving labor market conditions than counter-cyclical monetary and fiscal policies.

Chapter 3 – The unemployment rate greatly increased after the onset of the latest recession in December 2007, when it measured 5.0%. The rate peaked at 10.0% in October 2009, four months after the recession's official end in June 2009. More than three years into the recovery, the unemployment rate averaged 8.1% in 2012. Given its still elevated level, policymakers may continue to be concerned about how to spur economic growth and create jobs.

Over the past few years, Congress has used fiscal policy and the Federal Reserve (Fed) has used monetary policy to put the economy on a path toward the level of demand for goods and services that preceded the 2007-2009 recession. Firms react to recessions by laying off workers, and the deeper the downturn in the business cycle, the greater the rise in unemployment that results. Expansionary fiscal and monetary policies commonly have been used to remedy what is known as cyclical unemployment.

The unemployment rate has not been as responsive as had been hoped to the countercyclical measures undertaken by Congress and the Fed. Consequently, some have suggested that an increase in another type of unemployment—referred to as structural unemployment—has accounted for much of the rise in the unemployment rate from pre-recession levels. These observers assert that the rise in unemployment due to change in the structure of the economy represents "a new normal" of elevated unemployment rates for years to come.

Structural unemployment develops for different reasons than cyclical unemployment. Structural unemployment results when jobseekers do not move quickly into vacant jobs. Obstacles that lengthen the spell of unemployment (i.e., prolong the period of job search) include mismatches between the skills or locations of jobless workers and the skill requirements or locations of available jobs. Another impediment is the composition of the unemployed, such as more workers whose connection to their former employers is permanently severed (i.e., fewer workers likely to be recalled from layoffs once business revives at their former employers). A third factor that may contribute to long-term unemployment is known as labor market institutions, such as unemployment benefit programs.

The measures enacted by Congress have chiefly focused on alleviating cyclical unemployment. To the extent that the still-high unemployment rate results from the slow pace of output growth during the recovery, economic theory suggests that fiscal and monetary stimulus would be suitable strategies for further reducing joblessness. To the extent that structural factors have contributed to the still-high unemployment rate, economic theory suggests measures such as promoting the education and retraining of workers who permanently lost jobs in hard-hit industries (e.g., home building) so that they can acquire the skills needed to obtain employment in other industries.

This report assesses the relative magnitudes of cyclical and structural unemployment as they respond to different policy measures. An analysis of changes since 2007 in a variety of labor market indicators across industries and areas finds patterns that strongly suggest most of the increase in the U.S. unemployment rate is cyclical (i.e., due to depressed aggregate demand). Empirical studies suggest that, although structural unemployment has temporarily increased, it accounted for a minority of the rise in the unemployment rate in recent years.

In: The Labor Force Participation Rate
Editor: Darrel Graves
ISBN: 978-1-63463-391-8

Chapter 1

THE LABOR FORCE PARTICIPATION RATE SINCE 2007: CAUSES AND POLICY IMPLICATIONS*

Council of Economic Advisers

INTRODUCTION AND EXECUTIVE SUMMARY

In 2008, the U.S. economy collided with two historic forces. The first force was the Great Recession, the most severe economic crisis in a generation. While the economy has recovered considerably over the last five years, there is little doubt that more work remains to address some of the challenges left in the wake of the Great Recession. The turmoil of 2008 inflicted tremendous pain on millions of families, overshadowing the fact that 2008 also marked a unique milestone in U.S. economic history. That year, the first baby boomers (those born in 1946) turned 62 and became eligible for Social Security early retirement benefits. This second force—the demographic inflection point stemming from the retirement of the baby boomers—was felt far less acutely than the Great Recession, but will continue to have a profound influence on the economy for years to come, well after the business cycle recovery from the Great Recession is considered complete.

* This is an edited, reformatted and augmented version of a report issued by the Executive Office of the President, July 2014.

In addition to these inflection points in 2008, a number of longer-term trends had been playing out in the U.S. labor force prior to 2008—and have continued since then. These include the nearly continuous decline in labor force participation rates for prime-age males (i.e., age 25-54) since the mid-1950s and the dramatic rise in labor force participation rates for prime-age females in the 1970s and 1980s followed by a stalling and slight trend decline after the late 1990s.

Many dimensions of the economy's performance over the last several years can only be properly evaluated when the effects of the Great Recession, the retirement boom, and the longer-term labor force trends are taken into account. One of the clearest illustrations of this point is the labor force participation rate, which represents the fraction of the adult population either working or looking for work. Changes in labor force participation reflect not just current economic conditions like job availability and workers' assessments of job-finding prospects, but also more structural factors like the age distribution of the population and other aspects of society that impact people's decisions to participate in the labor force.

This report analyzes the evolution of the labor force participation rate since late 2007 and attempts to quantify the effects of these various forces. We examine the period since 2007 to focus on how each of the two largest forces, the Great Recession and the retirement of the baby boomers, has impacted labor force participation in recent years. We find that the combination of demographic changes and the drop in labor force participation that would have been expected based on historical business cycle patterns explain most but not all of the recent drop in labor force participation. This implies that other factors, likely including both a continuation of pre- existing trends in labor force participation by certain groups and the unique effects of the Great Recession have also been important. This report also discusses the labor force participation rates for different groups, discusses potential future scenarios for the participation rate, and lays out policies that would help to boost participation in the years to come.

Summary of the Main Results

Since the final quarter of 2007, the labor force participation rate has fallen from 65.9 percent to 62.8 percent in the second quarter of 2014, a decline of 3.1 percentage points. In this report, the Council of Economic Advisers estimates that this 3.1 percentage point decline can be attributed to three main sources:

About half of the decline (1.6 percentage point) is due to the aging of the population.

> Because older individuals participate in the labor force at lower rates than younger workers, the aging of the population exerts downward pressure on the overall labor force participation rate. While older workers today are participating in the labor force at higher rates than older workers of previous generations, there is still a very large drop-off in participation when workers enter their early 60s.

About a sixth of the decline in the overall participation rate (0.5 percentage point) is a cyclical decline in line with historical patterns in previous recessions.

> While the unemployment rate has come down from a peak of 10.0 percent in October 2009 to 6.1 percent in June 2014, it has remained elevated for the last several years. Historically, elevation in the unemployment rate is associated with a decline in labor force participation, as potential workers may decide to defer looking for a job until the economy improves. A portion of the most recent decline in the participation rate reflects this historical pattern, which this report refers to as the "cyclical" effect.

About a third of the decline (1.0 percentage point) arises from other factors, which may include trends that pre-date the Great Recession and consequences of the unique severity of the Great Recession.

In particular the two elements of this "residual" not explained by the standard factors are:

- The fact that participation rates conditional on age were declining for many groups in the run-up to 2008, including for prime-age men from the 1950s and for prime-age women from the late 1990s, may also have contributed to the decline in participation. This would have been expected to result in a decline in the participation rate above and beyond the pure aging effect even in the absence of a recession. Note, these effects were partly offset by other pre-existing trends, like a rise in the participation rate for older workers.

- The severity of the Great Recession, which has resulted in an unusual pattern of a very large share of long-term unemployed relative to total unemployment, may have lowered the participation rate more than would have been expected through normal channels. In fact, we find that a declining participation rate is historically correlated with the elevation of long-term unemployment, suggesting that both issues have a common cause or cause each other.

In the last few years the aging of the population has been an increasingly important source of the decline in the participation rate. From the beginning of 2011 to the second quarter of 2014, the participation rate fell by 1.4 percentage points. Around 70 percent of that decline (1.0 percentage point) can be directly attributed to the aging of the population and increased retirements.

Overview of the Report

Section I of this report provides historical context with a broad look at the participation rate since 1948. Then Section II surveys the literature on the participation rate in the Great Recession and subsequent recovery. Most researchers have found that long-term trends including the aging of the population explain a majority of the recent decline in participation, and that cyclical effects explain about a quarter of the decline. Section III explains CEA's decomposition of movements in the participation rate into the aging of the population, the business cycle, and other factors.

Section IV takes a deeper look at the trends in participation for several demographic groups: young men and women, older workers, prime-age women, prime-age men, and black men. Participation among young men and women has decreased steadily over the past decade, largely reflecting decreased participation among students and increased enrollment. Meanwhile, older workers have been participating at increasing rates over the last few decades. Black male participation has been on a troubling downward trend since the mid-1970s, falling about 10 percentage points over that time, while a similar, albeit slightly more muted decline has been seen among all men.

Section V lays out potential scenarios for the participation rate going forward assuming no policy changes are made. The aging of the population will likely continue to exert downward pressure on the overall participation rate. At the same time, continued recovery of the economy from the Great Recession would put upward pressure on participation. Assuming no change in policy we estimate that the recovery in the participation rate from cyclical factors will be roughly offset by the aging effect, leading to a mostly unchanged participation rate on net. However, it is difficult to know how much recovery in the residual will occur as the economy improves, and participation may rise as those additional workers are pulled back into the labor force. Once the cyclical rebound fades, however, assuming no policy or other structural changes, the participation rate will resume its downward trend driven mainly by aging. This discussion lays out a baseline for what might happen in the absence of policy steps to promote participation in the workforce.

Section VI lays out policy measures that can boost participation and in so doing, expand the economy's long-run growth potential. First, immigration reform would raise the size of the labor force as well as boost participation rates and could largely offset further declines in participation due to aging. Second, adopting family-friendly workplace policies can boost female labor force participation. For instance, many states are currently considering adopting paid leave policies, and evidence suggests that the availability of paid leave and other family-friendly policies could increase the participation of women by about 7 percentage points (Blau and Kahn, 2013). Third, the long-run decline in participation among men, especially minority men, is unsustainable, and the Obama Administration is aggressively pursuing policies aimed at stemming these declines. Finally, in the near-term, the recovery from the Great Recession remains incomplete, and steps to strengthen the economy and encourage best practices for hiring the long-term unemployed can still make a major difference. These types of steps are critical for combating the portion of the decline in the participation rate that reflects the unique severity of the Great Recession and the major challenges left in its wake.

I. The Labor Force Participation Rate over the Past 50 Years

The labor force participation rate is the share of the civilian population over age 15 that is either working or searching for work (i.e., unemployed). Increases in the participation rate reflect individuals joining the workforce, either by looking for a job or taking one, while decreases in the participation rate can reflect an increase in retirements, people taking time out of the labor force for a variety of reasons (e.g., to go to school, care for a young child, etc.), or unemployed individuals who become discouraged and stop looking for a job. Decreased labor force participation may or may not be desirable, depending on the reason. Achieving a labor force participation rate of 100 percent is not the goal, since many people who leave the labor force are engaged in important nonmarket activities, such as schooling, raising children, or retirement. However, discouraged workers dropping out of the labor force would be a cause for concern and would motivate enacting policies to return these workers to the labor force. In the long run, the growth rate of the labor force underpins the growth rate of employment, which, along with productivity growth, is a key determinant of the growth rate of potential GDP.

The labor force participation rate in the United States since 1948 has three key features, as shown in Figure 1. The first is the striking inverted U-shaped trend in the participation rate: while just under 59 percent of civilian adults were in the labor force in 1963, this rose to approximately 66 percent in 1990 and peaked at 67 percent in 2000, but since 2000 the participation rate has generally fallen. As discussed in more detail below, this inverted U-shaped pattern can be more fully understood by looking at the separate trends for men and women. In general, the left (rising) side of the inverted U-shape reflects a historic surge of women into the labor force in the second half of the twentieth century, as well as the baby boomers reaching their prime working years. The right (falling) side reflects the plateauing of female participation, combined with the retirement of the baby-boom generation and the massive shock of the Great Recession.

The second key feature of the participation rate visible in Figure 1 is the procyclical pattern. In other words, participation rises during an expansion and falls during a recession. For example, these cyclical patterns, which occur with a lag, are clearly visible in the 1990 recession. During the strong labor force growth of the 1970s and 1980s, the procyclical movements do not produce distinct declines in the participation rate, but instead produce temporary plateaus, as the cyclical decline was mitigated by an upward underlying trend that resumed after the recovery was under way. Similarly, because the participation rate was on a downward trajectory during the first half of the 2000s, the cyclical decline during and after the 2007 recession combined with the underlying demographic trend to produce a particularly sharp drop.

The third feature of the participation rate visible in Figure 1 is that the series exhibits considerable volatility around the long-term trends and cyclical movements. For example, during the recovery from the 1990 recession, the participation rate rose more than half a percentage point in the first half of 1992, only to subsequently fall by nearly the same amount. Much of this volatility stems from factors like the normal statistical noise that exists in any data series based on a limited sample and seasonally adjusted.

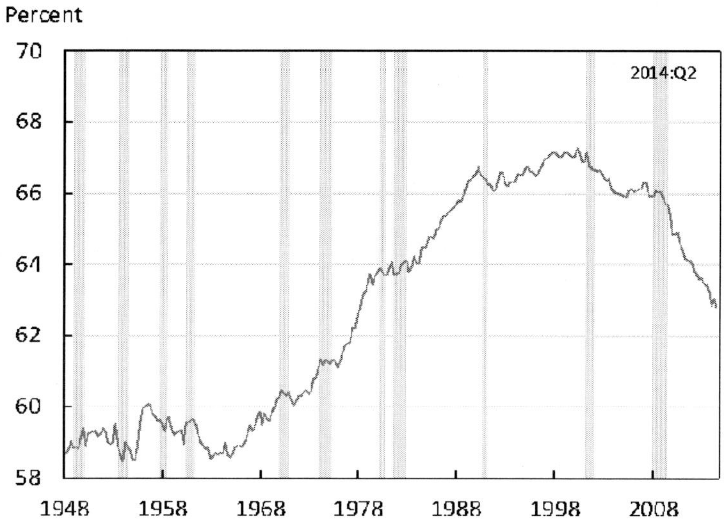

Figure 1. Total Civilian Labor Force Participation Rate.

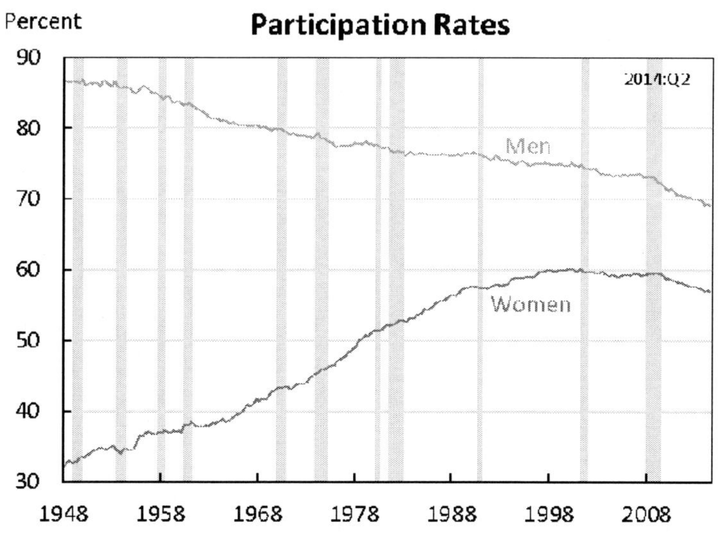

Figure 2. Male and Female Labor Force.

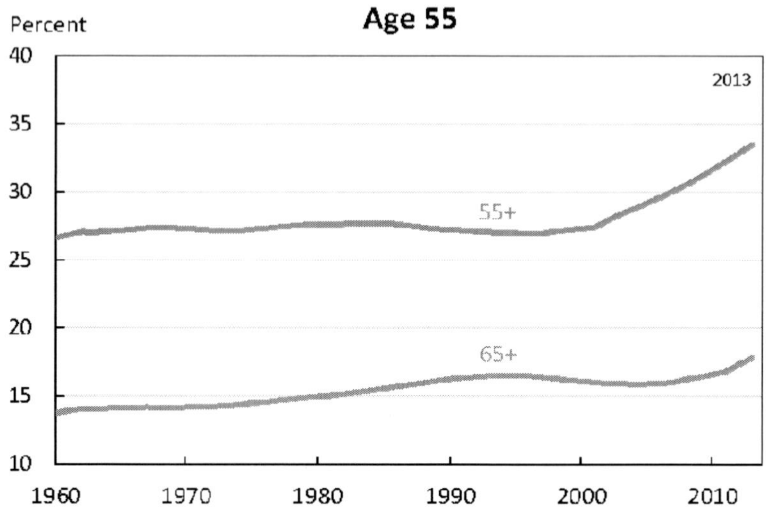

Figure 3. Share of the Adult Population Over.

As noted earlier, the inverted U-shaped trend in the overall participation rate can be better understood by considering the separate trends for male and female labor force participation. The male labor force participation rate has been falling since data collection began in 1948, as shown in Figure 2. Some of this decline reflects the increasing longevity of men over time and the resulting lengthening of their retirement. However, the rate of participation among prime-age men has also fallen over this time period, although to a lesser extent.

In contrast, women's labor force participation rose through much of that period, with a surge from the mid-1960s through the 1990s. This profound shift in America's economy and society reflected changes in social norms and access to education, including the legalization of oral contraceptives in the early 1960s, reductions in discrimination through legislation like Title VII of the Equal Rights Act and Title IX of the Educational Amendments to the Equal Rights Act, and developments in labor-saving household technology. The rise in women's labor force participation exceeds the decline in men's participation so that overall adult participation increased during this interval.

Since 2000, the participation rates of men and women have both declined, although the rate of decline has been slower for women than for men. Participation rates have long been influenced by an aging population, however its impact became more pronounced starting in 2008 when the first cohort of baby boomers (those born in 1946) turned 62 and became eligible for early Social Security benefits. Starting in 2008, the share of the working age population over age 55 began to rise rapidly (Figure 3). Also, while the share of the population over age 65 has risen gradually since 1960 due to increased longevity, the increase accelerated in 2008 and is now rising faster than at any point since 1960. This sharp and predictable retirement of a large cohort coincided with the start of the Great Recession, making it difficult to separate the effects of the economy and normal demographic patterns on participation. Even though these baby boomers are more likely to work at older ages than their predecessors, the employment rates at older ages are still much lower than for younger workers.

II. Literature on the Labor Force Participation Rate in the Great Recession and Subsequent Recovery

There has been considerable research on the decline in the participation rate in recent years. Table 1 lists the findings of several recent studies of the participation rate, showing how much of the decline each study attributes to long-term trends and cyclical factors. The time periods covered by each of these analyses vary, so the results are not always directly comparable—although we provide CEA's estimates to match the time periods of each of the studies. While some studies estimate either the trend or cycle component and then infer the other component indirectly, this table only shows direct estimates of these components.

Despite differences in data and methods, several broad conclusions are common across the literature. Taken together, the aging of the population and the business cycle account for the vast majority of the decline in the participation rate since 2007 in all of the studies. While there are some differences in the share attributed to the aging of the population, the median estimate is that half of the decline is due to aging.

CEA estimates that the long-term trend of an aging population explains just over half of the decline in participation since the end of 2007, putting CEA's estimate in the middle of the range of estimates. Across most of these studies, the effects of an aging population typically account for a third to half of the decline, and the other longer-term trends account for a varying proportion of the decline. The estimates of the trend component from

Aaronson et al. (2006), Kudlyak (2013), and Fallick and Pingle (2013) also include notable effects from other long-term trends, and so are correspondingly about 25 to 30 percentage points larger than estimates of the aging effects alone.

In analyzing the effects of the business cycle on participation, the literature is split between a group of analyses that attribute about 25 percent of the decline to the Great Recession and its aftermath, and a few studies that estimate the cyclical component to be at least a majority of the decline. Each paper takes a different approach to estimating the cyclical portion. Both CEA's estimate and Van Zandweghe (2012) are based on time series evidence but arrive at different conclusions.

Table 1. Comparison of Participation Rate Estimates

	Time Period	Shares of the Total Decline		CEA Estimated Shares of Total Decline over Same Time Period	
		Trend	Cycle	Trend	Cycle
CEA (2014)	2007:Q4 - 2014:Q2	52%	16%	--	--
Beginning in 2007					
Erceg & Levin (2013)	2007 - 2012	25%	60%	55%	35%
Shierholz (2012)	2007 - 2011	30%	--	50%	52%
Van Zandweghe (2012)	2007 - 2011	42%	58%	50%	52%
CBO (2014)	2007:Q4 - 2013:Q4	50%	33%	49%	20%
Fallick & Pingle (2013)	2007:Q4 - 2013:Q2	75%	16%	55%	29%
Aaronson et al. (2006)	2007 - 2013	80%	--	49%	20%
Kudlyak (2013)	2007 - 2012	80%	20%	55%	35%
Other Time Periods					
Aaronson, Davis & Hu (2012)	2000 - 2011	40%	--	46%	38%
Fujita (2014)	2000:Q1 - 2013:Q4	65%	30%	42%	16%
CEA (2014)	2011:Q1 - 2014:Q2	69%	-34%	--	--

Note: This table only includes direct estimates of the trend and cyclical components. CEA-equivalent decompositions for time periods listed on an annual basis are computed from Q4 to Q4 of the corresponding years.

While some studies recognize an unexplained or residual component of the decline in participation, others hold that the full decline in participation can be explained by a combination of longer-term trends and cyclical effects. CEA estimates that about one quarter of the decline is not explained by either trend or historical estimates of cyclical movements, but there is some evidence that this residual may be related to the current recession through its unusually high long-term unemployment rate. The Congressional Budget Office (CBO) estimates a slightly smaller residual component and suggests that it may be due to elevated Social Security Disability Insurance (SSDI) rolls. Other possible explanations for the residual component include increased enrollment in school (Fujita 2014).

III. Explaining the Decline in the Participation Rate Since 2007

CEA's analysis of the decline in the labor force participation rate since the end of 2007 is based on a variety of methodologies, including direct measurement of the aging trend, panel data, and time series analysis—all of which produce generally similar results in disentangling three effects: the pure aging effect, the standard cyclical effect, and a residual which picks up a combination of pre-existing trends unrelated to aging and factors unique to the Great Recession.

The Aging of the Workforce

The largest single factor in the decline of the participation rate since the end of 2007 is the aging of the workforce—something that was predicted well before the Great Recession. Every year since 2000, the Economic Report of the President has mentioned the post-2008 decline in the labor force participation rate as a factor slowing growth of potential real GDP. In 2004, the first year in which their ten-year forecast included the 2007-2013 period, CBO predicted that participation would fall by 1 percentage point between 2007 and 2013 due to aging. Also, in 2006 researchers from the Federal Reserve predicted, based solely on aging and other trends, that the participation rate would fall to 63.3 percent in 2013—the exact value to which it fell (Aaronson et al. 2006).

Labor Force Participation over the Life Cycle

Labor force participation varies considerably over the course of a person's life, rising rapidly at early ages before flattening out through the working years and falling as workers retire. In order to understand how an aging population will affect overall labor force participation, it is helpful to look at how the participation rates of different age groups have changed over time. Figures 4 and 5 show the participation rates for men and women over the course of their lives for various birth cohorts. For both men and women, participation rises rapidly throughout the 20s as individuals leave full-time schooling and enter the workforce, then flattens out at a high level during prime working-age years, before falling to low levels of participation again as individuals enter their 60s. In the decade leading up to age 65, participation for both men and women falls by at least 40 percentage points, and continues to fall by nearly 20 percentage points over the subsequent decade of the life cycle.

The pattern of participation among prime-age women has shifted dramatically over the past half century. Women born in 1933 decreased their participation over the course of their 20s—the ages of maternity and childrearing--before slowly increasing their participation in their 30s and 40s. The cohort of women born ten years later, in 1943, had much the same pattern of decreasing and increasing participation, but over the course of their lifetime participated at a rate about five to ten percentage points higher. In subsequent cohorts, women participated at much higher rates in their 20s and 30s, while participation rose only slightly in older years. Most of this increase is likely due to women in more recent cohorts returning to the labor force more quickly after bearing children than previous generations.

Male participation has shown less variation from cohort to cohort, but there are two notable changes. The first is that among prime working-age men, each successive cohort has participated slightly less on average, demonstrating that the long-run decline in male participation has been partially driven by the behavior of prime-age men. The second is that more recent cohorts of older men have increased their participation. Men born in 1943 participated at age 65 at a rate about five to ten percentage points higher than men born in 1933. It is also worth noting that men born in 1943 had a life expectancy roughly 5 years longer than those born in 1933. Despite this increase in participation relative to previous cohorts, there is still a very large drop off in participation at older ages, and so an aging population will, all else equal, reduce the economy- wide labor force participation rate. The substantial aging of the population that has begun to occur and will continue to unfold for years to come is discussed in the next subsection.

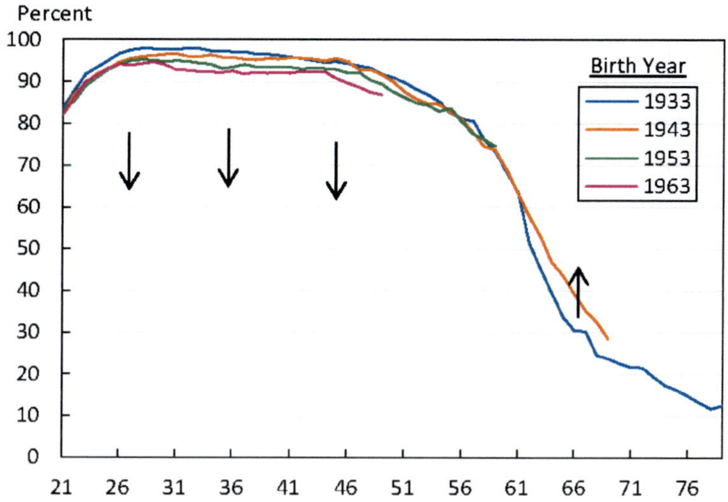

Figure 4. Male Labor Force Participation by Age & Birth Year.

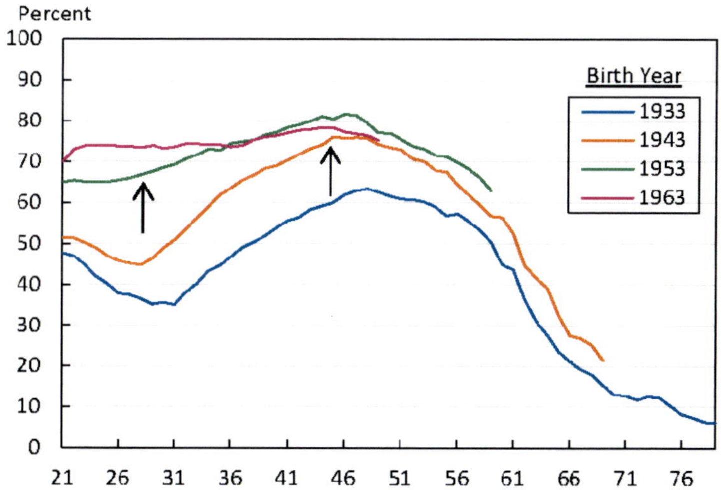

Figure 5. Female Labor Force Participation by Age & Birth Year.

Aging and the Retirement of the Baby Boomers

In the immediate aftermath of World War II, the U.S. birth rate spiked, as couples who were reunited following the war were able to settle down and have children, while others took advantage of the relative sense of peace and prosperity that emerged in the 1950s and 1960s to expand their families

(Figure 6). The birth rate remained elevated into the mid-1960s before dropping sharply, and it has not since returned to anywhere close to what it was during the baby boom. Consequently, the baby boomers, who are currently between the ages of 49 and 67, are more numerous than any previous or subsequent cohort of Americans.

As Figure 7 shows, the distribution of the population by age becomes more heavily tilted toward older ages as the baby boomers age. The first baby boomers reached retirement age in 2008, and over the next decade and a half, increasingly-large cohorts of baby boomers will follow suit. In 2009, 16 percent of the adult population was at or above the retirement age; the Social Security Administration projects this fraction will grow to 25 percent by 2029, increasing by half over two decades.

The retirement of the baby boom generation is particularly consequential for the participation rate, because the labor force participation rate falls sharply as workers grow older. Both men and women decrease their participation by at least 40 percentage points in the decade leading up to age 65, and participate at even lower rates afterwards. Because older individuals participate in the labor force at lower rates than other age groups, the shift in the age structure from aging baby boomers is responsible for a substantial portion of the decline in the participation rate.

Figure 6. U.S. Birth Rate.

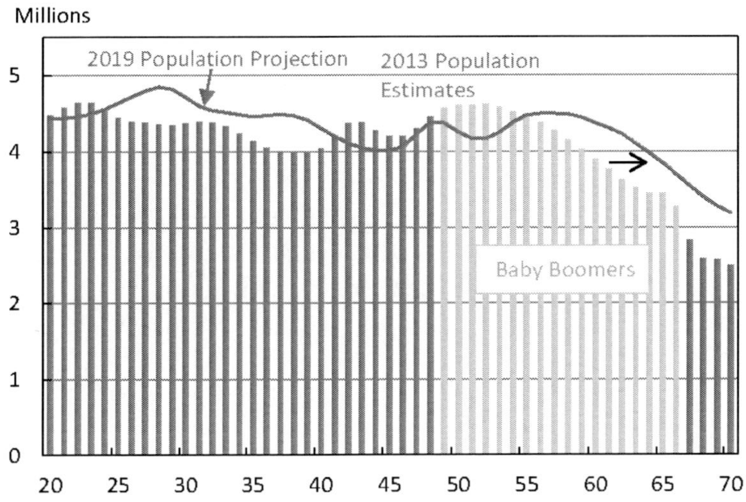

Figure 7. U.S. Population Distribution by Age.

Although the participation rate of those over age 60 has risen in recent years and the participation of older baby boomers is continuing to rise relative to previous cohorts, this effect is relatively small compared to the typical decline as people age and so does little to mitigate the substantial negative effect that aging of the population has on the overall participation rate. The participation rate for the male cohort born in 1943 fell more than 40 percentage points as they aged from 55 to 65, even though their participation was about 10 percentage points higher than those in the previous cohort at age 65. The pattern for women is largely similar, as the increase in participation at older ages from cohort-to-cohort is much smaller than the drop in participation over the lifecycle.

Modeling the Effect of Aging on the Participation Rate

Two longer-term trends contribute to movements in the participation rate: first, the effect of an aging population, and second, ongoing trends in participation within age groups that are unrelated to aging. The magnitude of the trend can be estimated in several ways, each of which captures long-term movements in participation differently, with some capturing only the effects of aging and others including both aging and non-aging-related trends. We employ three different methods of modeling the participation rate trend and find that they provide similar estimates, with approximately half of the decline in participation since 2007 attributable to aging and a negligible fraction of the decline attributable to trends within age groups.

Projecting Forward the 2007 Participation Rate Profile with Changing Age Structure

A straightforward way to estimate the effect of the aging of the population on labor force participation is to hold constant the participation rates by age in a given year, and observe how the participation rate evolves if only the age distribution of the population is allowed to vary. For example, this allows computing the effect of an increasing share of 65 year olds, under the assumption that 65 year olds retire in the future at the same rate that they did in 2007. This approach is implemented using the age-based participation profile as of 2007. The advantage of fixing participation rates in 2007 is that it predated the recession, and thus avoids confounding the analysis by introducing the further effect of a sharp cyclical movement. However, the results are essentially the same if we instead hold the current (2014) participation rates by age group constant, as discussed later.

To estimate the effect of aging, we constructed data on participation rates for single-year age categories by gender, combining unpublished participation rates for those over 55 with participation for single-year age categories below age 55 obtained by interpolating from the published rates for ten-year age categories. For individuals above age 55, data on annual participation by single-year age category were provided to us by the Bureau of Labor Statistics (BLS), using unperturbed data from the Current Population Survey (CPS). These data are less noisy than estimates from the CPS microdata but are not very different on average (Appendix Figures 1 and 2).

Figure 8 shows the counterfactual participation rate between 2007 and 2014, under the assumption that only the age distribution of the population changed over this time. Over this period, the counterfactual participation rate fell by 1.6 percentage points, accounting for slightly more than half of the actual observed decline.[1] Thus, the aging of the population alone can explain about half the decline in the participation rate since late 2007.

The aging portion of the trend has been more rapidly declining since 2011. Between the end of 2007 and the end of 2010, the counterfactual participation rate fell only 0.6 percentage point, but it subsequently fell 1.0 percentage points from the beginning of 2011 through the first quarter of 2014—explaining the majority of the reduction in participation over that period. In 2011, the first baby boomers reached age 65, which is the point of steepest decline in participation over the lifecycle. Baby boomers will continue to turn 65 until 2029 and the aging portion of the trend in the participation rate will correspondingly continue to decline, possibly at an even more rapid pace in the coming years.

Casselman (2014) conducts a similar calculation using the publicly available data on participation published by BLS and concludes that aging is responsible for about a third of the decline. However, the seasonally adjusted statistics published by BLS categorize all adults over 55 into the same group, which obscures significant differences in participation at older ages. Participation falls by about 40 percentage points between age 55 and 65, so compositional shifts within the 55+ age group can have a large effect on the overall participation rate; using the coarse age- bracket data will not capture this effect. In contrast, the analysis here enables an estimate of a more detailed, year-by-year aging effect.

Time Series Trend

Econometric analysis of time series data can also be used to estimate the long-run trend in the participation rate. Unlike the previous approach that was designed to isolate the effect of population aging, this approach identifies a single unified trend in the participation time series and so does not separate aging and non-aging forces driving the trend. Although the theory of time series trend estimation is well-developed, this application is challenging because the deep recession and prolonged recovery serve to conflate the cyclical and trend behavior beginning in late 2007. For this reason, the time series trend used here is estimated using a standard time series smoother (biweighted kernel), modified to be cyclically adjusted using a partially linear semiparametric model; more detail is given in Appendix A. The resulting estimate shows that the trend component of the participation rate peaked in the late 1990s, and has been falling since, declining at a more rapid rate in recent years (Appendix Figure 3). According to the time series estimate of the trend, the long-run trend in the participation time series fell by 1.6 percentage points between the end of 2007 and the second quarter of 2014.

The 1.6 percentage point decline in the time series trend happens to equal the estimated decline in the previous section that focused on the aging-based trend. Since the time series model includes trends within age groups while the aging-based trend does not, by itself this estimate would suggest that non-aging trends within age groups have had little net effect on participation. However, in the presence of a break in the series—which we know occurred around 2008 with the retirement boom—time series methods will tend to understate the trend. As a result, the residual between the time series and aging methods will tend to understate the consequences of pre-2008 trends unrelated to aging.

Structural Micro-Data Models of Participation

Another approach to estimating the trend in participation involves estimating a structural model of participation decisions using individual-level data. This approach was originally developed by Aaronson et al. (2006), who extend the model with age and cohort effects to include covariates representing human capital, the ability to finance nonparticipation spells, and family structure. By including a measure of life expectancy, for example, the authors control for longer lives requiring greater retirement savings, which in turn would increase participation. In contrast to the previous two methods, this approach attempts to ascertain the separate effect of various factors driving differences in participation across individuals and across cohorts. Aaronson et al.'s projections, which assumed full employment, were consistent with a decline in the participation rate from 2007:Q4 through 2014:Q2 of 2.5 percentage points. If this is correct, then most of the decline in participation since the end of 2007 would have been foreseeable—and in fact was almost precisely foreseen—based on pre-existing trends in aging and other demographic factors.

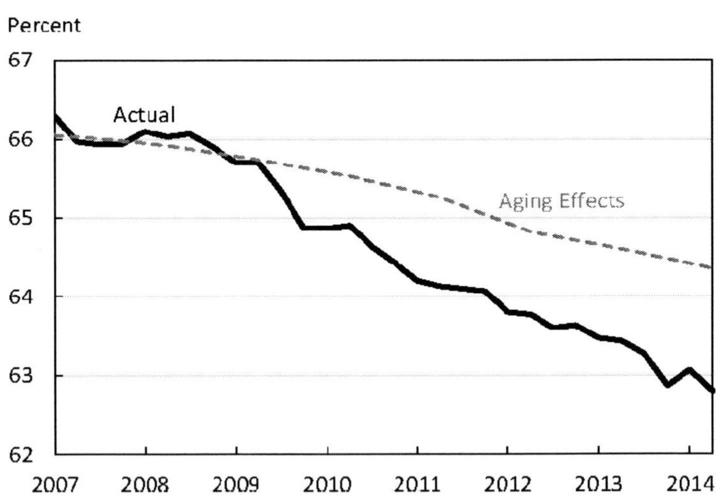

Figure 8. Effect of Aging on Labor Force Participation.

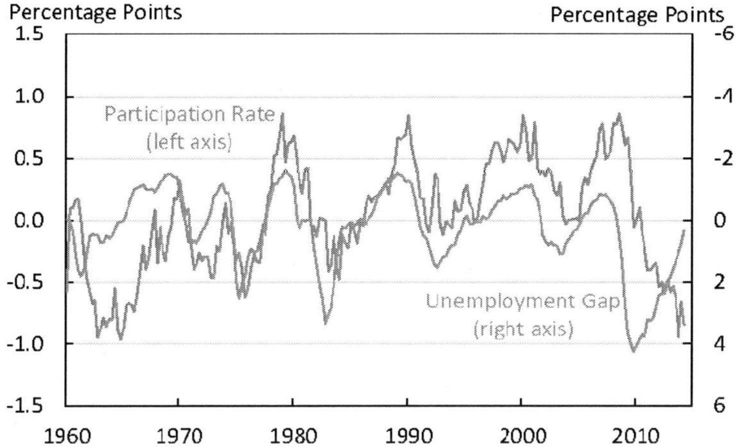

Figure 9. Detrended Participation Rate and (Inverted) Unemployment Gap.

Fallick and Pingle (2007) propose a more detailed structural model of participation. They use several covariates to estimate the trend in participation, including educational attainment, life expectancy, marriage and fertility variables for women, minimum wages and school enrollment measures for teenagers, and Social Security rule changes. In a recent update of their model using data collected in the years following publication, they estimate that the participation rate trend decreased 2.0 percentage points between the end of 2007 and the second quarter of 2014. Fallick and Pingle's model includes some portion of what we estimate as cyclical rather than trend components, however, because several of the covariates they include exhibit cyclical variation (in particular the return to education and the level of private wealth). To the extent that their estimated trend component is based on variables that fluctuate cyclically, their estimate arguably overstates the portion of the decline attributable to long-term trends.

Standard Business Cycle Effects

The decline in the labor force participation rate since 2007 is partially due to the standard effects associated with an economy operating below its full potential. However, because the shock of the Great Recession was so large, the standard cyclical effects on participation were also quite large relative to previous cycles. When the economy is booming, the labor force participation rate rises and often exceeds the predicted long-term trend, and during downturns the participation rate falls below trend. Economic contractions historically result in both greater unemployment and lower labor force participation, as nonparticipants become less likely to enter the labor force and the unemployed (who always exhibit a higher tendency to exit the labor force) become more numerous relative to the employed (Elsby, Hobijn, and Sahin 2013). While movements in the participation rate over decades are driven largely by the long-term trends, in the short-and medium-term the variation in the participation rate is driven by these cyclical factors.

Figure 9 shows the cyclicality of the participation rate by comparing the detrended participation rate and the detrended unemployment gap, defined as the difference between the actual unemployment rate and the natural unemployment rate (to simplify comparison, the unemployment gap is plotted inverted)[2]. For example, in the expansion of the 1990s, the detrended participation rate rose, and during the Great Recession, the detrended participation rate declined. Visual inspection suggests that movements in the participation rate lag, by perhaps a year or so, movements in the unemployment rate, a phenomenon discussed in more detail below. The cyclical pattern of the participation rate is also evident when looking at state-level data, where the states with the largest increases in unemployment tended to have larger declines in labor force participation (Figure 10). Roughly speaking, for every percentage point increase in the unemployment rate, the participation rate falls by about 0.2 percentage point, a pattern that has roughly held over the last four recessions (Figure 11).

While it is possible to estimate a cyclical effect on participation using microdata, the studies in the literature that have tried this approach have produced cyclical estimates that do not comport with the dynamics evident in the total participation time series (Bengali, Daly, and Valletta 2013; Erceg and Levin 2013). The cyclicality of participation varies significantly across the population, with participation among younger workers being highly cyclical and participation among prime- age workers hardly responding to the business cycle. Alternatively, one can estimate the cyclical component indirectly by subtracting the trend component from the observed participation rate and treating this entire residual as the cyclical component (Van Zandweghe 2012). However, this approach does not distinguish between the typical cyclical response from a severe recession and the decline in participation coming from challenges unique to the Great Recession and its aftermath.

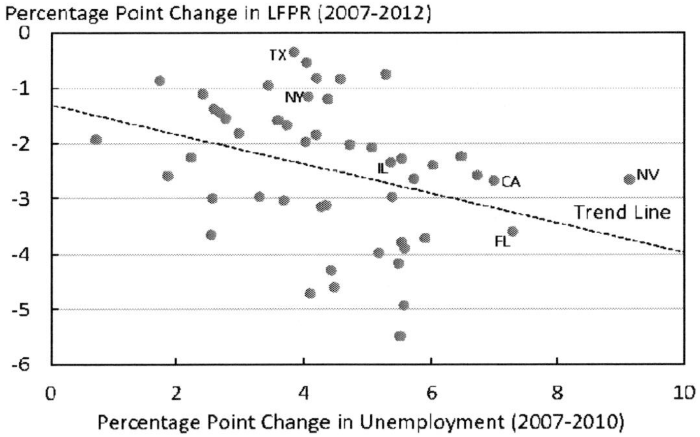

Figure 10. Labor Force Participation and Unemployment by State.

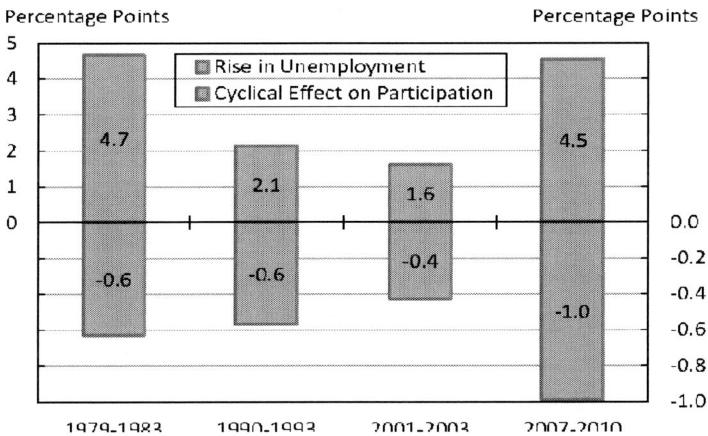

Figure 11. Cyclical Declines In Labor Force Participation.

In this report, we estimate the cyclical component using econometric analysis of time series data, where the cycle is defined by the unemployment gap. We consider two alternative distributed lag specifications, one in which the detrended overall participation rate is regressed on the level of the detrended unemployment gap and its lags, and a second in which the quarterly first difference of the detrended overall participation rate is regressed on the four-quarter difference of the detrended unemployment gap and its lags. The regression results for the two methods are summarized in Tables 2 and 3, respectively.

Table 2. Levels on Levels Regressions using the Unemployment Gap

Variables	Detrended Participation Rate, 16+			
	(1)	(2)	(3)	(4)
Unemp. Gap	-0.0142 (0.0615)	**-0.120**** (0.0530)	0.165 (0.121)	0.140 (0.126)
Unemp. Gap (t-1)			**-0.216**** (0.0957)	-0.191* (0.102)
Unemp. Gap (t-2)			0.0184 (0.0607)	0.0298 (0.0649)
Unemp. Gap (t-3)			-3.71e-05 (0.0889)	-0.110 (0.0798)
Unemp. Gap (t-4)	**-0.140***** (0.0428)		-0.138 (0.0853)	0.0451 (0.0686)
Unemp. Gap (t-5)				-0.0773 (0.0729)
Unemp. Gap (t-6)				0.0652 (0.0622)
Unemp. Gap (t-7)				-0.0858 (0.0884)
Unemp. Gap (t-8)	-0.0462 (0.0378)			-0.00831 (0.0854)
Constant	0.0840 (0.0870)	0.0619 (0.0902)	0.0761 (0.0863)	0.0821 (0.0878)
Observations	210	218	214	210
F-test of Included Coefficients	**8.530**	**5.143**	**6.075**	**4.006**
Prob > F	2.29e-05	0.0243	2.84e-05	9.99e-05
F-test of Restricted Coefficients	1.919	**3.551**	2.248	
Prob > F	0.0793	0.000719	0.0652	
Predicted Cyclical Decline (2007:Q4 -2014:Q2)	-0.477	-0.113	-0.465	-0.486

Note: Regressions are estimated using data from 1960:Q1 to 2014:Q2. Newey-West standard errors using a maximum lag of 12 are reported in parentheses. Participation rate and unemployment gap are detrended using the procedure described in Appendix A. F-tests of restricted coefficients are the joint significance test of the omitted coefficients all equaling zero in a regression with all eight lags (i.e. in regression (3),it tests the hypothesis that the coefficients on the unemployment gap in t-5 through t-8 are all equal to zero).

*** p<0.01, ** p<0.05, * p<0.1

Several results are evident in Tables 2 and 3. First, in the specifications with the full set of eight lags, many of the coefficients are individually statistically insignificant. However, restricting the lag structure to allow only the contemporaneous unemployment rate to enter (regressions (2) and (6)) is rejected at the 5 percent significance level. But once lags are introduced, some restrictions are consistent with the data: one of the specifications with shorter lags (3) and both specifications with the contemporaneous, fourth, and eighth lag ((1) and (5)) are not rejected at the 5 percent level. Moreover, the predicted values from regressions (1), (4), (5), and (8) are largely the same (Appendix Figure 4). Thus, the predicted results are largely robust across the non-rejected specifications. An important distinction between the first-difference and levels specification is that the levels specification imposes the restriction that the long-term forecast of the labor force participation rate reverts to its long-term trend, whereas the differences specification permits a persistent gap between the long-term trend line and the participation rate (so that in effect the trend shifts up or down to match permanent shifts in the level of the participation rate). In the current situation, this distinction corresponds to whether the gap between the labor force participation rate and its cyclical component (the residual) will entirely disappear, or whether that gap might persist because of the labor market disruptions of the Great Recession. We view this as an empirical question, and to avoid imposing the additional mean-reverting structure on the cyclical component, we adopt the first-difference specification. Further, to reduce estimation noise we adopt the restricted-lag specification; this reasoning leads us to choose (5) as our preferred specification. Note, however, that the decomposition results are not particularly sensitive to these choices because varying them yields similar estimates of the cyclical components.

The predicted path for the participation rate, combining our estimate of the time series trend with our preferred specification (regression (5) in Table 3), is shown below in Figure 12. We estimate that between 2007 and 2014:Q2, business cycle effects alone explain 0.5 percentage point (about one sixth) of the total fall in the participation rate.

With the improvement of the labor market, the usual cyclical drag on participation due to elevated unemployment is declining. We estimate that, as of 2011, the participation rate was 0.9 percentage point lower because of cyclical factors. By 2014:Q2, however, the cyclical portion had shrunk to 0.5 percentage point because the unemployment rate has fallen. The drop in the cyclical contribution corresponds to nearly 1 million workers returning to the labor force because of cyclical reasons since 2011.[3]

Table 3. Differences on Differences Regressions using the Unemployment Gap

Variables	Quarter-to-Quartaer Difference of Detrended Participation Rate, 16+			
	(5)	**(6)**	**(7)**	**(8)**
Year-over-Year Difference of Unemp. Gap	**-0.0340***** (0.00891)	**-0.0355***** (0.00783)	0.0105 (0.0239)	0.0259 (0.0292)
Year-over-Year Difference of Unemp. Gap (t-1)			-0.0689 (0.0500)	-0.107* (0.0551)
Year-over-Year Difference of Unemp. Gap (t-2)			-0.00142 (0.0578)	0.0459 (0.0573)
Year-over-Year Difference of Unemp. Gap (t-3)			0.0545 (0.0468)	-0.00622 (0.0536)
Year-over-Year Difference of Unemp. Gap (t-4)	**-0.0187**** (0.00740)		**-0.0473**** (0.0204)	0.0630 (0.0514)
Year-over-Year Difference of Unemp. Gap (t-5)				**-0.131**** (0.0637)
Year-over-Year Difference of Unemp. Gap (t-6)				0.0899* (0.0531)
Year-over-Year Difference of Unemp. Gap (t-7)				-0.0491 (0.0508)
Year-over-Year Difference of Unemp. Gap (t-8)	-0.00563 (0.00751)			0.0179 (0.0393)
Constant	-0.00141 (0.00731)	-0.00289 (0.00836)	-0.00371 (0.00807)	(0.00754) -0.00162
Observations	210	218	214	210
F-test of Included Coefficients	**11.74**	**20.52**	**9.623**	**6.686**
Prob > F	3.90e-07	9.74e-06	2.81e-08	2.34e-08
F-test of Restricted Coefficients	1.872	**2.590**	**2.422**	
Prob > F	0.0873	0.0103	0.0496	
Predicted Cyclical Decline (2007:Q4 - 2014:Q2)	-0.507	-0.303	-0.544	-0.474

Note: Regressions are estimated using data from 1960:Q1 to 2014:Q2. Newey-West standard errors using a maximum lag of 12 are reported in parentheses.

Participation rate and unemployment gap are detrended using the procedure described in Appendix A. F-tests of restricted coefficients are the joint significance test of the omitted coefficients all equaling zero in a regression with all eight lags (i.e. in regression (3),it tests the hypothesis that the coefficients on the unemployment gap in t-5 through t-8 are all equal to zero).

*** p <0.01, ** p <0.05, * p <0.1

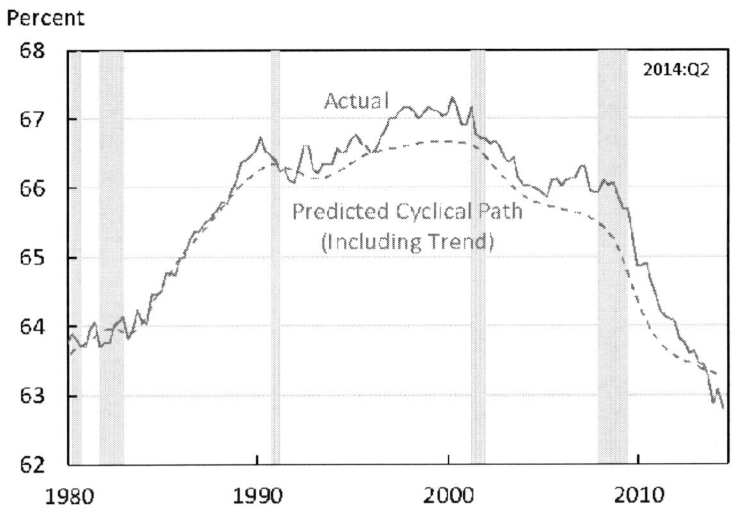

Figure 12. Estimated Trend Plus Cyclical Component of the Labor Force Participation Rate, 1980-2014.

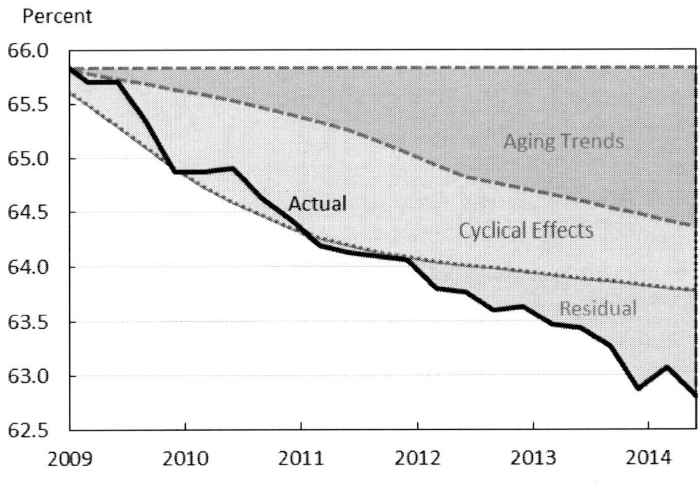

Figure 13. labor Force participation Decomposition.

Other Effects on Participation: Non-Aging Trends and Factors Unique to the Great Recession

Most of the decline in participation since the end of 2007 is accounted for by the aging of the population and the standard cyclical effects associated with the elevated unemployment rate. The remaining reduction in the participation rate—a 1.0 percentage point reduction in the participation rate since the end of 2007—is not explained by either of these two previously discussed factors.

This residual is a relatively recent phenomenon in this recovery. Up until the beginning of 2012 the participation rate was generally slightly higher than would have been predicted based on the aging trend and the standard business cycle effects. But in the last two years, the participation rate has continued to fall at about the same rate even though the unemployment rate has been declining rapidly. This means that the standard cyclical effect has been giving way to a growing unexplained residual (Figure 13).

The literature has put forward several possible explanations for this residual component which fall mainly into two categories: long-term trends within age groups and factors unique to the Great Recession. We cannot precisely break down these two factors. At least some of the residual appears to be these pre-existing trends, many of which are discussed in the next section about different demographic groups, although some of these pre-existing trends are partially offsetting (e.g., prime-age male labor force participation was already falling while older workers were seeing a rising participation rate). The fact that the residual only emerged later in the recovery suggests that much of it might be the result of factors specific to the Great Recession and its aftermath. We focus here on testing three unique factors of the Great Recession that may be linked to the residual component, but other forces may also explain the residual decline.

Significantly Elevated Long-Term Unemployment

The Great Recession has led to an unprecedented increase in long-term unemployment, with the number of individuals unemployed for 27 weeks or more rising from 1.3 million at the end of 2007 to more than 6 million at the end of 2010. Even though the rate of short-term unemployment (26 weeks or less) has since returned to its 2001-07 average, the long-term unemployment rate remains more than double what it averaged during the previous expansion.

The emergence of a large residual in our participation rate model coincides with a sustained elevation of the long-term unemployment rate, suggesting that these two phenomena could be different manifestations of the same underlying challenge, or that one is causing the other. To test the plausibility of this hypothesis, we look at the historical relationship between the residual (unexplained component) and the extent of long-term unemployment. Specifically, we ran several regressions using the detrended mean duration of unemployment as a regressor in addition to the detrended unemployment gap that was used in the standard cyclical estimates above.[4] As Tables 4 (levels on levels) and 5 (differences on differences) show, the mean duration of unemployment was highly statistically significant in the differences specification but only marginally significant in the levels specification. These tables also show the effects of disability insurance and school enrollments, which will be discussed below.

Using these regression results, we can predict the path of the participation rate given the large increase in the mean duration of unemployment since 2007. Estimating this new set of additional factors explains much of the previously unexplained decline in participation since 2009, as seen in Figure 14. This suggests that the unusually high rate of long-term unemployment may be exerting downward pressure on the participation rate—or that these two developments are manifestations of a common underlying cause.

One theory put forward to explain the rise in long-term unemployment during the most recent recession is that the long-term unemployed are less productive workers on average and will take longer to find new jobs (Cowen and Lemke 2011). However, the long-term unemployed appear similar to the short-term unemployed in many dimensions, including gender, educational attainment, and previous industry and occupation (Mitchell 2013; Krueger, Cramer, and Cho 2014). Lower productivity among the long-term unemployed could be related to unobservable characteristics, but it is not clear whether the differences among unobservable traits are large enough to explain the rise in long-term unemployment.

A more plausible explanation for the rise in long-term unemployment is that firms are screening out applicants based on duration of unemployment. Long-term unemployed workers are about half as likely to get a callback for an interview as equally-qualified short-term unemployed workers (Kroft, Lange, and Notowidigdo 2013). Short-term unemployed applicants with no relevant work experience for a particular job are more likely to be interviewed for the job than long-term applicants with relevant work experience (Ghayad 2013). Workers who are not lucky enough to find a job within the first few months of unemployment will face disadvantages in the hiring process, further lengthening their unemployment spells on average and raising the rate of long-term unemployment.

Table 4. Levels on Levels Regressions using Disability Claims, Duration of Unemployment, and Enrollment Rate

Variables	Detrended Participation Rate, 16+					
	(1)	(2)	(3)	(4)	(5)	(6)
Unemployment Gap	-0.0142 (0.0723)	-0.0712 (0.0805)	-0.0130 (0.0574)	-0.0154 (0.0597)	-0.00373 (0.0619)	0.0153 (0.0640)
Unemp. Ga p (t-4)	**-0.140***** (0.0525)	**-0.169**** (0.0654)	**-0.142***** (0.0417)	**-0.137***** (0.0455)	**-0.137***** (0.0431)	**-0.135***** (0.0404)
Unemp. Ga p (t-8)	-0.0462 (0.0609)	0.0249 (0.0569)	-0.0512 (0.0425)	-0.0499 (0.0453)	-0.0332 (0.0402)	-0.0453 (0.0468)
Mea n Duration of Unemp.	-8.35e-06 (0.0224)	0.0400 (0.0279)				
Mean Duration of Unemp. (t-4)		-0.0356 (0.0296)				
Mea n Duration of Unemp. (t-8)		-0.0119 (0.0242)				
SSDI Claims			**0.000933**** (0.000468)	0.000615 (0.00115)		
SSDI Claims (t-4)				0.000272 (0.00188)		
SSDI Claims (t-8)				0.000121 (0.00124)		
Enrollment Rate					-22.92 (19.18)	-41.04 (32.51)
Enrollment Rate (t-4)						5.962 (27.62)

Variables	Detrended Participation Rate, 16+					
	(1)	(2)	(3)	(4)	(5)	(6)
Enrollment Rate (t-8)						26.26 (39.03)
Constant	0.0840 (0.0892)	0.0842 (0.0900)	0.0860 (0.0881)	0.0859 (0.0881)	0.0997 (0.0799)	0.0892 (0.0792)
Observations	210	210	204	204	210	210
F-test	1.38e-07	2.624	**3.974**	0.157	1.429	0.379
Prob > F	1.000	0.0750	0.0476	0.855	0.233	0.685

Note: Regressions are estimated using data from 1960:Q1 to 2014:Q2. Newey-West standard errors using a maximum lag of 12 are reported in parentheses. Participation rate and unemployment gap are detrended using the procedure described in Appendix A. F-tests are joint significance tests of the disability insurance, mean duration, and schooling variables.

*** p <0.01, ** p <0.05, * p <0.1

Table 5. Differences on Differences Regressions using Disability Claims, Duration of Unemployment, and Enrollment Rate

Variables	Quarter-to-Quarter Difference of Detrended Participation Rate, 16+					
	(7)	(8)	(9)	(10)	(11)	(12)
Year-over-Year Difference of Unemp. Gap	**-0.0297***** (0.00890)	**-0.0330***** (0.00914)	**-0.0322***** (0.00989)	**-0.0321***** (0.00992)	**-0.0330***** (0.00884)	**-0.0328***** (0.00877)
Year-over-Yea r Difference of Unemp. Gap (t-4)	-0.0130 (0.0103)	0.00429 (0.0146)	**-0.0228**** (0.00943)	-0.0149 (0.0111)	**-0.0181**** (0.00724)	**-0.0190**** (0.00737)
Year-over-Year Difference of Unemp. Gap (t-8)	-0.00350 (0.00776)	0.0151 (0.0114)	-0.0117 (0.00916)	-0.0170* (0.00901)	-0.00481 (0.00786)	-0.00569 (0.00744)

Table 5. (Continued)

Variables	Quarter-to-Quarter Difference of Detrended Participation Rate, 16+					
	(7)	(8)	(9)	(10)	(11)	(12)
Year-over-Year Difference of Mean Duration	-0.00387 (0.00436)	-0.00406 (0.00534)				
Yea r-over-Year Difference of Mean Duration (t-4)		**-0.0142***** (0.00524)				
Year-over-Year Difference of Mean Duration (t-8)		0.00222 (0.00527)				
Yea r-over-Year Difference of SSDI Claims			0.000546 (0.000614)	-0.000610 (0.000874)		
Yea r-over-Year Difference of SSDI Claims (t-4)				0.00120 (0.00117)		
Year-over-Yea r Difference of SSDI Claims (t-8)				-0.000719 (0.000756)		
Year-over-Year Difference of Enrollment Rate					-2.510 (4.275)	-2.910 (4.702)
Year-over-Year Difference of Enrollment Rate (t-4)						2.876 (4.415)
Year-over-Year Difference of Enrollment Rate (t-8)						0.444 (3.391)
Constant	-0.000523 (0.00743)	0.00247 (0.00676)	0.00154 (0.00658)	-0.00225 (0.00698)	-0.00124 (0.00732)	-0.00147 (0.00719)
Observations	210	210	145	137	210	210

Variables	Quarter-to-Quarter Difference of Detrended Participation Rate, 16+					
	(7)	(8)	(9)	(10)	(11)	(12)
F-test	0.789	**3.529**	0.788	0.373	0.345	0.161
Prob > F	0.376	0.0159	0.376	0.773	0.558	0.923

Note: Regressions are estimated using data from 1960:Q1 to 2014:Q2. Newey-West standard errors using a maximum lag of 12 are reported in parentheses. Participation rate and unemployment gap are detrended using the procedure described in Appendix A. F-tests are joint significance tests of the disability insurance, mean duration, and schooling variables.

*** $p < 0.01$, ** $p < 0.05$, * $p < 0.1$

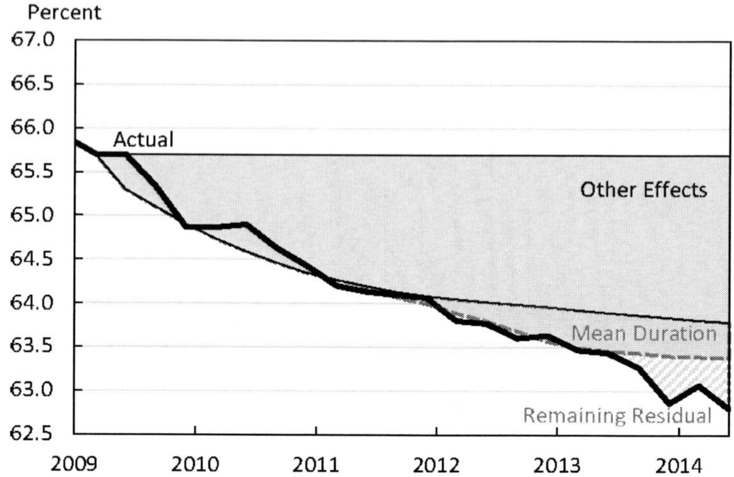

Figure 14. Labor Force Participation Decomposition Including Mean Duration of Unemployment.

Recent research finds that the period of elevated long-term unemployment that we are experiencing is consistent with historical patterns after adjusting for the deeper decline and slower recovery from the latest recession (Kroft, Lange, Notowidigdo, and Katz 2014). Consistent with the fact that the long-term unemployed are observably similar to the short-term unemployed, Kroft et al. find that demographics, occupations, industries, regions or reasons for unemployment do little to explain the variation in unemployment spell length. Instead, they attribute a large share of the rise in long-term unemployment to negative duration dependence, meaning that as a spell of unemployment persists, it becomes more likely to persist even longer. They further find that changes the flows between unemployment and non-participation in the labor force account for another large share. They allow that the long-term unemployed may be unobservably less productive, but their two favored explanations leave little unexplained.

Disability Insurance

Since the end of 2007, the number of disabled workers receiving benefits through the Social Security Disability Insurance (SSDI) program has increased by nearly 2 million. Some have argued that changes in Disability Insurance are causing an unusual decline in the participation rate. However, we find little evidence that the increase in Disability Insurance beneficiaries explains the residual component of the decline in participation. We estimated a series of regressions using the detrended time series of Disability Insurance disabled worker beneficiaries as an additional explanatory variable. Tests of the coefficients were mostly statistically insignificant and only barely significant in one specification (regression (3) in Table 4). Looking at the predicted values from these regressions, the estimated path of participation accounting for Disability Insurance did not fit the historical series substantially better than our preferred specification using only the unemployment gap.

Disability Insurance generally increases when the unemployment rate increases. As such, the increase in Disability Insurance beneficiaries is captured in our estimate of the cyclical effect and does not appear to have had a disproportionate effect in recent years. In terms of this decomposition, Disability Insurance does not appear to explain the residual component of the decline in the participation rate.[5]

In fact, if anything, the increase in disability rolls since 2009 have been somewhat *lower* than one would have predicted given the predicted cyclical and demographic effects, although it is still within a 95 percent confidence interval (Figure 15).

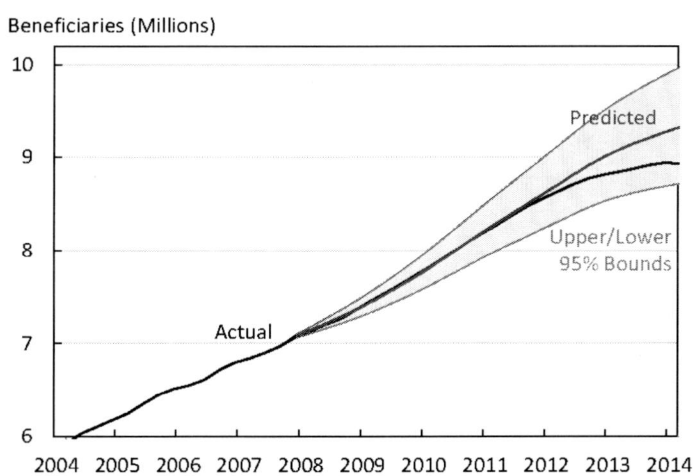

Figure 15. Predicted SSDI Beneficiaries.

Schooling

Young men and women are increasingly enrolling in school full-time instead of entering the labor force. The effects of the Great Recession have further encouraged young workers to enroll in school and delay entering the labor force. However, school enrollment tends to be counter- cyclical and therefore any effect of a typical increase in schooling during a recession is already included in our estimate of the cyclical component. If the increase in school enrollment between 2007 and 2014 is larger than the typical increase during a recession, though, it may explain some of the residual decline in participation.

We estimate several regression specifications in both levels and differences using the percent of the population enrolled in high school or college as an additional explanatory variable. As Tables 4 and 5 show, the enrollment rate is not statistically significant in any of the specifications we estimate. Analyzing the cyclical patterns in the enrollment rate itself reveals that the dynamics of enrollment between 2007 and 2014 are largely in line with the expected path given the counter-cyclical nature of enrollment in the past.

It is important to note that this analysis only captures the effect of changes in enrollment decisions, and not changing participation conditional on enrollment. Students enrolling in school participate at lower rates than their non-enrolled peers, so a higher enrollment rate leads to lower participation on average. However, the participation of students enrolled in school has been on a downward trend since 2000, which accounts for a portion of the decline in participation among younger workers. This implies that the participation decisions of young workers may have changed in ways that are not fully captured in the enrollment rate. However, when looking at the overall participation rate, this change is part of the other offsetting trends discussed in greater detail below.

IV. Changes in Labor Force Participation for Different Demographic Groups

Overall, the major *aggregate* trend affecting the participation rate in the recession and recovery is the aging of the population. But there are a number of important trends and developments for different subgroups of the population. For example, we have seen declining participation by younger Americans as they stay in school longer, increasing participation by older Americans, a plateauing of, and subsequent slight decline in, female labor force participation in the last fifteen years following earlier increases, and the continuation of a 65-year trend of declining male labor force participation (which is especially stark for young minority men).

Table 6 shows the trends for a wide range of groups and the remainder of this section discusses trends for some of the specific groups.

Young Men and Women

Labor force participation among young workers (16-24 year olds) is at its lowest level in more than 50 years, having fallen steadily since its peak in the late 1980s, and is now 15 percentage points lower than it was 30 years ago, as seen in Figure 16. However, given the relatively small size of this group, this trend has had a much smaller impact on the overall labor force participation rate. Since 2007, participation among young people has fallen by about 0.8 percentage point per year, while school enrollment has increased. Enrollment has risen since the 1980s with larger increases in enrollment among lower-income households, as shown in Figure 17. As a result, the share of young people who are either in the labor force or in school has largely been unchanged.

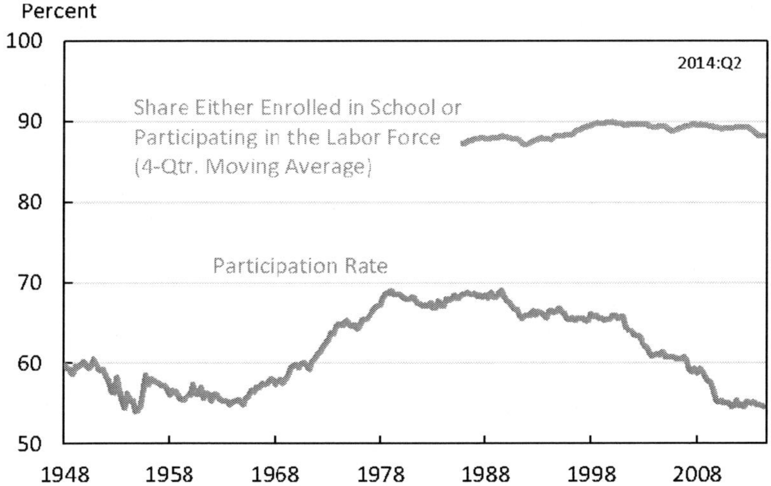

Figure 16. Labor Force Participation Rate of 16-24 Year Olds.

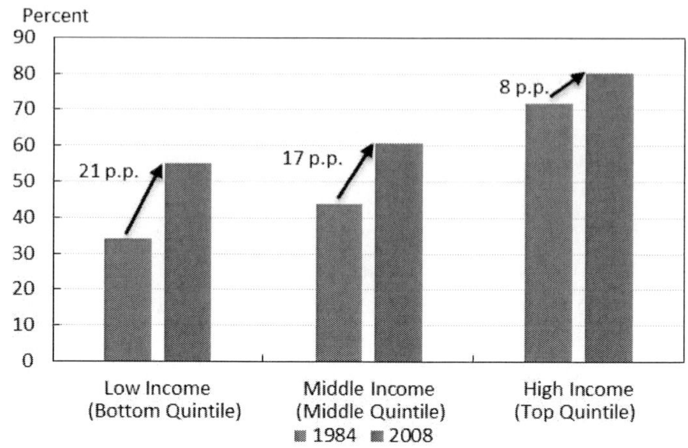

Figure 17. Postsecondary Enrollment of High School Graduates by Income.

Aaronson, Park, and Sullivan (2006) examine the secular decline in teen (16-19 year olds) employment dating back to the mid-1980s and hypothesize that teens are responding to the rise in returns to college by enrolling in school. They find that most of the decline in employment between 1987 and 1997 was due to a rise in school enrollment, but since then most of the decline is due to reduced participation among young people enrolled in school. Over the last two decades, the share of 16-24 year olds neither enrolled in school nor participating in the labor force has not changed significantly, ticking down slightly from 11.9 percent in 1993 to 11.7 percent in 2013. The lack of any increase in the share neither enrolled nor participating implies that the decline in the 16-24 year old participation rate since 1993 has come from a reduction in participation among 16-24 year olds enrolled in school. Indeed, the participation rate of 16-24 year olds enrolled in school has declined more than 10 percentage points over the past two decades.

Two main factors have likely played a role in the increase in enrollment since 1980, which accounted for much of the decrease in participation among the young between 1980 and the mid-1990s. First, increased subsidies for college combined with higher returns to staying in school have changed the economic calculus around schooling decisions. Second, a reduction in middle-skilled jobs (which economists have referred to as job "polarization") has led less-skilled adult workers to push teenage workers out of the labor force.

Table 6. Participation Rate by Selected Groups

	2014-Q2	Change (per year in p.p.)		
		1948-1990	1990-2007	2007-2014
All	62.8	0.2	0.0	-0.5
Men	69.1	-0.2	-0.2	-0.6
Women	56.9	0.6	0.1	-0.3
16-24	54.7	0.2	-0.4	-0.8
25-54	80.8	0.5	0.0	-0.3
55+	40.0	-0.3	0.5	0.2
Men 25-54	88.0	-0.1	-0.1	-0.5
Women 25-54	73.9	1.0	0.1	-0.2
White*	63.1	0.2	0.0	-0.5
Black**	60.9	0.3	0.0	-0.5
Hispanic***	65.8	0.5	0.1	-0.5
Black Men**	63.3	-0.1	-0.2	-0.5
Black Women**	58.9	0.6	0.1	-0.4

* Series begins in 1954

** Series begins in 1972

*** Series begins in 1973.

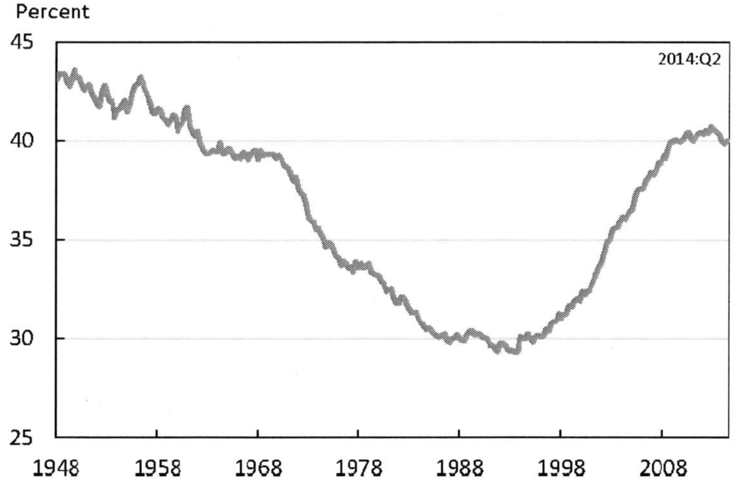

Figure 18. Labor Force Participation Rate of 55+ Year Olds.

Smith (2011) examines the decline in the teen (16-19 year olds) employment-population ratio which has been trending down since the mid-1980s, steepening in the recent period since early 2000s. Using cross-state analysis, the author finds a significant negative relationship between changes in teen employment and the fraction of adults in jobs that often employ teens such as low-wage service sector jobs. Job polarization—declining middle-skilled jobs and growing low- wage jobs—may have resulted in increased competition between less-skilled adult workers and teenage workers. The author finds that such explanations can account for over half of the cyclically-adjusted decline in teen employment since the mid-1980s. It is plausible that these forces have grown over the recent recession as youth, particularly teens, faced greater competition for jobs from more experienced adults who were laid-off (Fogg and Harrington 2011).

Older Workers

After many decades of decline, labor force participation rates among older workers have stabilized since the 1980s and have started to increase in recent years (Figure 18). Participation among older women was largely flat for several decades before experiencing an unprecedented increase over the last two decades, rising more than 10 percentage points. This rise in the labor force participation for older workers has been attributed to several factors. Maestas and Zissimopoulos (2010) and Blau and Goodstein (2010) identify rising education levels, labor force participation of wives, and changes in Social Security as the most important factors leading to the reversal in the trend. While there is less direct evidence available, it seems likely that improvements in health and increases in life expectancy have also played a role.

The increase in participation by older workers is partially due to differences in the skills that they acquired when they were younger. Between 1876 and 1950, the average years of schooling for each birth-year cohort increased steadily every year, according to Goldin and Katz (2007). The increased education among each successive cohort meant that retirees in more recent years have had more income and better quality, less physically demanding jobs over the course of their lives (Maestas and Zissimopoulos 2010). Blau and Goodstein (2010) estimate that at least 15 percent of the increase in labor force participation since 1988 can be attributed to the rising education levels in each successive cohort, but their robustness checks indicate that this may be an underestimate and rising education might in fact explain the entire increase in participation among older workers since 1988.

Another portion of the recent rise in participation among married men has come from the increased labor force participation of their wives. The rise in female labor force participation since the late 1980s explains about a quarter of the rise among older men (Blau and Goodstein 2010, Schirle 2008). This effect is likely due to complementarity of leisure time between husbands and wives, where retirement is more appealing if one's spouse is also retired. Couples tend to retire at similar times and men's retirement decisions are very responsive to the incentives faced by their wives (Coile 2004).

Additionally, there have been a number of policy changes to the Social Security program since 1980, and these policies may have had an effect on the retirement decisions of older workers. In particular, research in this area has centered around two types of policies: changing the level of full benefits and changing the timing of when full benefits are paid out. Changes in the generosity of benefits appear to have had little effect on the labor supply of older workers, while changes in the timing of full benefits account for much of the increase in participation at older ages (Blau and Goodstein 2010, Gustman and Steinmeier 2008). In particular, the increase in the Normal Retirement Age and the creation of the Delayed Retirement Credit (that is, the increase in benefits from working past the normal retirement age) together can explain between a quarter and half of the increase in labor force participation among older workers since 1988 (Blau and Goodstein 2010).

There appears to be, as yet, little in the way of rigorous empirical studies examining two factors which likely contributed to the recent rise in participation among older workers: improvements in health and technology. Improvements in health can enable workers to continue to work later in life and the corresponding increase in longevity will raise the amount of saving needed for retirement. Additionally, technological improvements can also help accommodate older workers in the workplace.

As older workers have delayed retirement and increased their participation in the labor force, there has been a rise in partial retirement as a means of shifting gradually from the lifestyle of prime working years to retirement (Maestas 2007). According to Maestas, most of these retirees anticipated working in retirement, and retirees who unexpectedly return to the labor force typically do so because they find leisure less enjoyable than they expected. Additionally, older workers are increasingly likely to be self-employed (Maestas and Zissimopoulos 2004). About 25 percent of all 65 year old workers are self-employed, and of these workers more than 40 percent have employees working for them (Maestas and Zissimopoulos 2010).

Between 1990 and 2007, participation among workers over 55 grew by an average of 0.5 percentage point per year, but this slowed to 0.2 percentage point per year since 2007 (Table 6). Our analysis of the over 55 participation rate suggests that the increase since 2007 was not driven by the Great Recession, and in fact we estimate that the cyclical downturn actually slightly decreased the participation of older workers relative to what it would have otherwise been. Research on the effects of the Great Recession is largely in line with this result, finding that wealth shocks were concentrated in wealthier households, and as a result did not substantially alter retirement decisions in recent cohorts (Gustman, Steinmeier, and Tabatabai 2011).

Prime-Age Women

The labor force participation rate for prime-age women rose rapidly from around 1970 through 2000. This rapid rise was driven by many factors coming together: reductions in discrimination facilitated by Title VII of the Civil Rights Act and Title IX of the Educational Amendments to the Civil Rights Act, the availability of more effective birth control through the invention and subsequent legalization of the birth control pill, and changes in economic forces stemming from the greater educational gains of women, the advent of labor-saving household technology, and increased international trade. While these changes drove participation in the 1970s and 1980s, further increases in the 1990s stemmed from the incentives provided by the expansion of the Earned Income Tax Credit (EITC), the replacement of Aid to Families with Dependent Children (AFDC) with the work-centered Temporary Assistance for Needy Families (TANF), and reforms to divorce laws. But the participation rate has since levelled out, as seen in Figure 19. As a result, the United States has gone from leading many other European countries in prime-age female labor force participation to lagging them (Figure 20).

Research has found that family-friendly policies are partially responsible for the rise in participation in other advanced countries, and the lack of these policies explains why the United States has lost ground. Policies such as paid parental and sick leave, high quality available daycare, and support for part-time work have been enacted in other advanced countries, enabling mothers to more easily balance work and family obligations. Blau and Kahn (2013) investigated data on participation across developed countries and found that the lack of family- friendly policies in the United States can explain roughly a quarter of the relative decline in women's participation between 1990 and 2010.

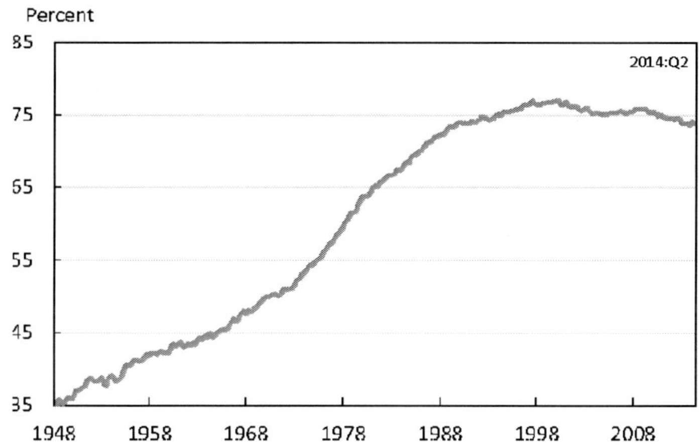

Figure 19. Labor Force Participation Rate of 25-54 Year Old Women.

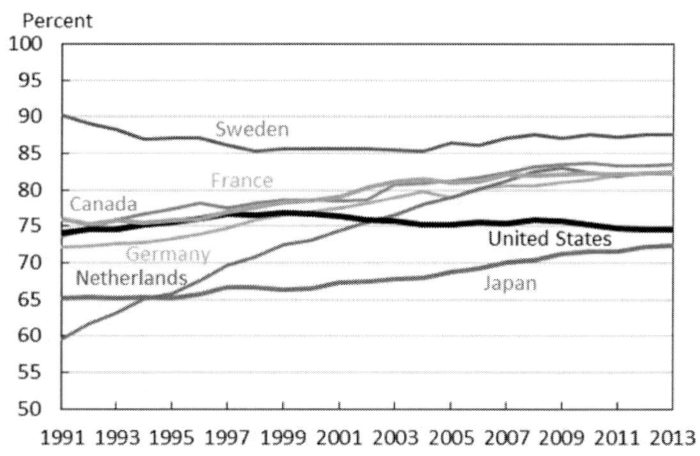

Figure 20. Labor Force Participation Rate of Women Aged 25–54, 1991–2013.

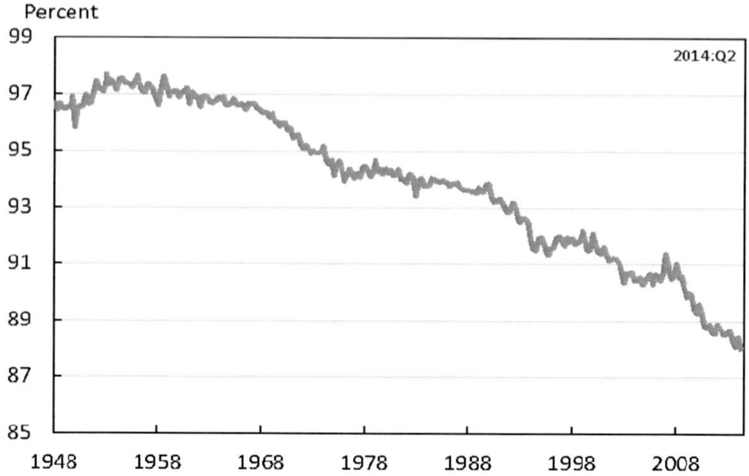

Figure 21. Labor Force Participation Rate of 25-54 Year Old Men.

Access to paid family leave is a particularly important factor for mothers considering whether or not to remain in the labor force, since it enables mothers to continue working for an employer after giving birth. In 2004, California became the first State to implement a paid family leave program. Rossin-Slater, Ruhm, and Waldfogel (2013) examined the decisions of mothers before and after the program's implementation, finding that it significantly boosted the number of hours that mothers worked two to three years after giving birth. They also find that the program reduced the number of mothers without jobs, although this effect was not quite statistically significant. Other research on paid leave programs has shown that access to paid leave increases the likelihood that a recent mother will return to her employer in the United States, the United Kingdom, and Japan (Waldfogel, Higuchi, and Abe 1999), although a study of paid leave in Norway found no effect on labor force participation, perhaps reflecting stronger pre-existing work supports (Dahl et al. 2013).

At the same time as the participation rate for women has stagnated, the role of women in the workforce has continued to grow in importance. More and more women are working in traditionally male-dominated occupations and becoming breadwinners for their families: married women now contribute almost half of family earnings. This is in part because young women are now more likely than young men to have graduated from college, and the share of female students enrolling in MD, JD, and MBA programs has grown to nearly 50 percent for each of these degrees.

Prime-Age Men

There has been a steady decline in the labor force participation of prime-age men since the 1950s (Figure 21). In 1950, 92 percent of prime-age men were employed, while the most recent data show that the percentage has fallen to 83 percent, in other words a decline of nearly 10 percent. This decline in part reflects the fact that prime-age men have historically been more concentrated in jobs that can be replaced by technology or sent overseas. As described in Goldin and Katz (1998) and Autor, Katz, and Kearney (2008), skill-biased technological change has long exerted an influence on the wage structure by depressing wages for occupations with manual or routine labor. As Autor, Dorn, and Hanson (2013) note, these effects are concentrated among industries exposed to foreign competition and international trade.

There is some disagreement in the literature on whether SSDI accounts for a part of the participation decline, particularly for lower-skilled male workers. Wage stagnation for less- educated workers have made Social Security benefits increasingly valuable compared to low- wage workers' earnings, and reforms passed in 1984 increased SSDI receipt, although this increase may have reflected the fact that the level of SSDI receipt was temporarily depressed before 1983 and subsequently returned to its normal level after reforms were enacted (Autor and Duggan 2003, Pattison and Waldron 2013). As discussed above, more recent growth in the program has been driven mostly by demographics and the recession.

Regardless of the source, the prolonged decline in participation among prime-age men is worrying because this group has historically comprised the largest share of the workforce. Even seemingly modest declines in their participation cumulate over long periods of time and result in large changes in the numbers of Americans available for work, and this in turn has predictable negative effects on growth.

Black Men

Black male labor force participation has fallen steadily since the mid-1970s, dropping more than 10 percentage points over that time. In part, this reflects lower education levels among black men, only 47 percent of whom today have at least some college education (compared with 57 percent for white men). For both black and white men, labor force participation has fallen more for those with lower education levels. At the same time, however, the decline in participation has been greater for black men across the education spectrum. Participation among black workers with just a high school degree has declined nearly 10 percentage points over the last decade, while the participation rate among black college graduates has declined by 3.5 percentage points; this compares with 4.6 percentage points and 2.7 percentage points declines for white men, respectively. This troubling trend of reduced participation has continued in the latest business cycle, with the participation rate for black men down 0.5 percentage point per year since the end of 2007 (Figure 22).

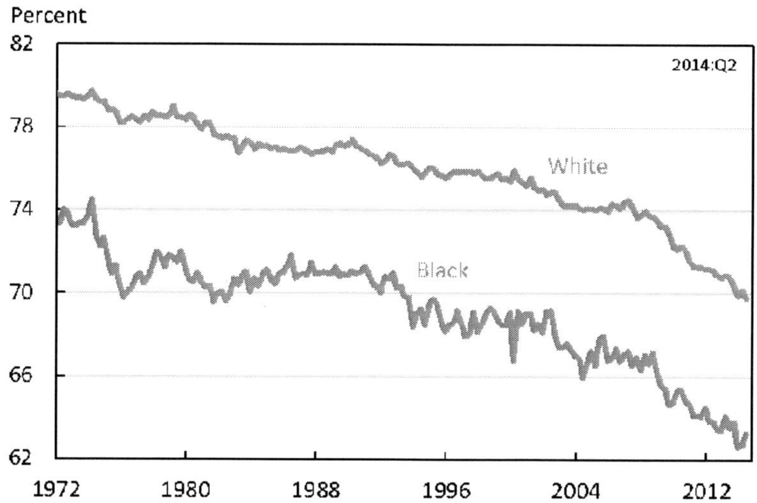

Figure 22. Male Labor Force Participation Rates by Race.

The decline in black male participation, which has persisted through both recessions and recoveries, has long been the subject of research (Moynihan 1965, Bound and Freeman 1992). The decline has also been particularly pronounced among the young: while the participation rate of older black men is also below average, theirs is higher than that of young black men, who have a lower labor force participation rate than young white and Hispanic men. This persistent gap between black men and their peers in participation and employment opportunities more generally is likely due to a range of factors such as disparities in family life and education, as well as employer attitudes and the structure of the labor market (Danziger and Gottschalk 1995, Bound et al 1995, Juhn 1992, 2003, Chandra 2003, Bertrand and Mullainathan 2003).

Over the last decade or so, labor force participation among black men has deteriorated even further. One of the leading explanations for this development is the steep rise in incarceration of young black males. Freeman (2003) estimated that roughly 20 percent of the black male population is incarcerated. In addition to the obvious incapacitating effect of current incarceration, even previous incarceration can have a negative effect on labor force activity. For one, incarceration tends to weaken employment networks (Travis, Solomon, and Waul 2001). Moreover, an audit study of employers in Milwaukee by Pager (2003) suggests that employers seem much more averse to hiring black males with criminal records than comparable white men, and that this deterrence extends even to those without criminal records (Holzer, Raphael, and Stoll 2002, 2006). These demand-side factors serve to reinforce supply-side factors that keep black men out of the labor market.

Holzer, Offner, and Sorenson (2005) test this hypothesis in their analysis of black males ages 16-34 with a high school education or less in the 1980s and 1990s. They find that previous incarceration can account for a quarter or more of the decline in participation among black males ages 16-24 and at least half of the decline among black males ages 25-34. These estimates of the effects of incarceration are corroborated by work by Western and Pettit (2000).

V. The Outlook for the Participation Rate

Assuming a continuation of current policies, over the longer term the participation rate will continue to trend down as the aging of the population continues. Over the next few years, however, it is likely that the continued recovery of the economy will tend to push in the other direction from the aging trend. The evolution of the residual component of participation is harder to predict given the uncertainty about its exact cause. All told, over the next few years, the participation rate could rise or fall slightly—followed by a resumption of its longer-term decline due to the continued aging of the population. Policy has the ability to affect these trends as we discuss in Section VI.

While the first baby boomers became eligible for early Social Security benefits in 2008, the last baby boomers will not reach this point of their lives until 2026. The share of the population over the age of 55 will continue to grow rapidly during the coming decade, and most of this growth will be in the share of the population over the age of 65 (Figure 23). While the share of the population over age 65 has risen gradually in the past due to increased longevity, the retirement of baby boomers accelerated this growth and it is now rising faster than at any point since 1960. If the participation profile by age were fixed at 2013 levels, the changing population share would subtract about 0.2 percentage point per year from the participation rate through 2024.

As the economy has recovered from the Great Recession, the cyclical drag on the participation rate has lessened to about 0.5 percentage point in the second quarter of 2014. As the economy continues to return to full employment, this cyclical factor will continue to dissipate. If this gap were to be closed over about two years, then the dissolution of the cyclical drag on participation would add about 0.2 percentage point per year to the participation rate for the next two years— roughly offsetting the aging trend.

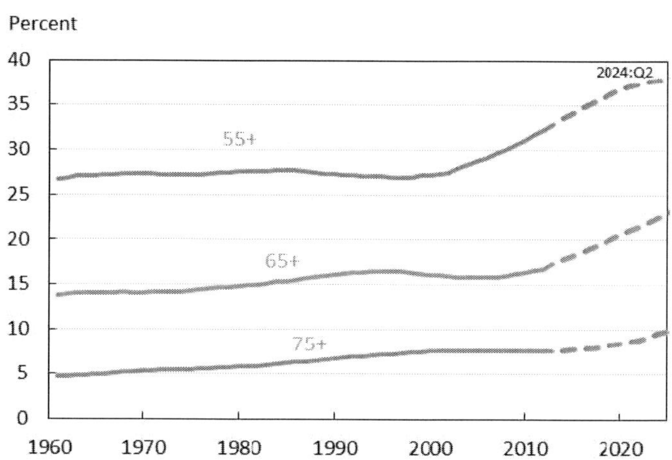

Figure 23. Older Worker Share of the Population.

The residual component of the decline in participation represents the greatest source of uncertainty about the participation rate going forward, in part reflecting the uncertainty about its causes. This component may shrink to zero, reflecting temporary factors dissipating as the economy recovers. On the other hand, to the degree it represents trends that pre-date the Great Recession, then absent policy shifts or other unexpected developments it could persist or even grow larger—Aaronson et. al (2006) projected that it would reduce the participation rate by 0.2 percentage point per year above and beyond the normal aging trend. Moreover, while long-term unemployment and other indicators of labor market challenges have been steadily improving, there is always a danger that without policy changes some individuals would permanently drop out of the labor force, resulting in a participation rate that would be permanently lower as a result. It also remains possible that the residual could grow over the next few years, as it has grown considerably over the past few years and may continue to do so in the near future.

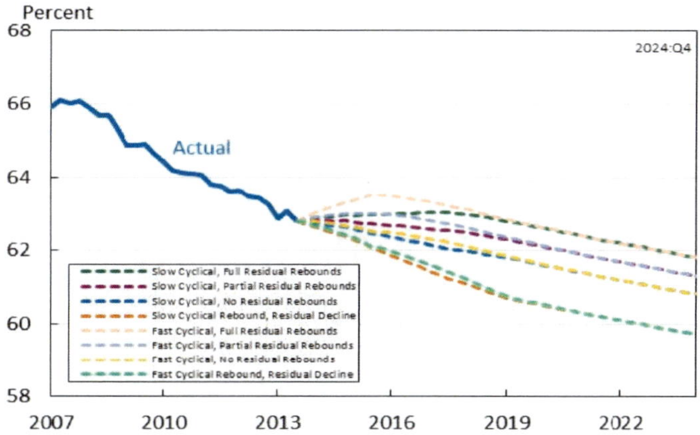

Figure 24. Alternative Scenarios for the Participation Rate.

Ultimately, absent changes in policies, a meaningful increase in the participation rate from current rates appears unlikely. Figure 24 shows several scenarios for the participation rate under current policies, with a common assumption about the aging trend but varying assumptions about the evolution of the cyclical and residual components discussed above. These scenarios are not projections and do not represent the full range of possibilities, but they do indicate that the participation rate is likely to be roughly stable in the near term and will decrease more rapidly after the economy returns to full employment and the aging effects once again dominate.

VI. The President's Agenda and the Labor Force Participation Rate

The outlook for the participation rate, however, ultimately depends, at least in part, on policy choices that we make and the practices adopted by companies and individuals. We discuss some of the major policies the Administration is pursuing to improve the trajectory of the participation rate here.

Aging of the Population

It is important to put the aging trend in perspective. That older workers are able to retire is in many ways a positive development. But it also creates challenges, especially for overall fiscal policy and in particular for programs like Social Security and Medicare.

Part of the answer to these challenges is enabling older workers who want to continue to work to do so. Workplace flexibility policies that allow employees to work part-time or flexible hours can help older workers tailor their jobs to their specific needs and can create roles that are less demanding than full-time employment. In this year's State of the Union, the President called on employers to expand access to flexible workplace policies. For similar reasons, many older workers choose self-employment, opting to retire partially or set their own hours. Many other older workers would like to be self-employed, but have medical conditions that make health insurance a necessity. Although in the past these workers would have had to seek work at a large employer offering health insurance coverage, the Affordable Care Act enables these workers to become self-employed by providing access to quality, affordable health insurance (Fairlie, Kapur, and Gates 2011) until they are eligible for Medicare.

Probably the most significant policy response to falling labor force participation rates is immigration reform, which would counteract the labor force effects of an aging population and spur economic growth. On average, immigrants are younger and participate in the labor force at higher rates than native-born Americans.

The Congressional Budget Office (2013) estimates that the immigration reform bill passed by the Senate would increase the labor force by 6 million people, or five percent, by 2023, and raise the labor force participation rate by 0.7 percentage point. This trend would continue over time, providing a range of other economic benefits such as increasing GDP, lowering budget deficits, and improving Social Security solvency.

Trends within Demographic Groups

Policies can also help address the long-term trends in participation within age groups. The participation rates for prime-age men and women have declined steadily over the past decade, continuing a decades-long trend among men and reversing a decades-long trend among women. Among younger workers, participation rates have fallen more rapidly. The fall in participation among young black men has been particularly drastic. The President's agenda addresses these trends and lays out a series of policies that could help encourage individuals to remain in the labor force.

To encourage more women to participate in the labor force, the Administration has a robust policy agenda around working families, which was further developed at the White House Working Families Summit in June 2014. The summit brought together government, private- sector, labor, and academic leaders to discuss how to help workers balance their personal and professional lives. Policies such as paid family leave, flexible work schedules, and affordable childcare are vital for families, and mothers in particular. Such policies not only encourage participation in the labor force, but they also help people find the jobs best suited to their skills and excel in those positions. Given that women often take on well over half of family obligations, such policies are particularly helpful in raising women's labor force participation (Blau and Kahn 2013). As women now make up nearly half of the labor force and earn 59 percent of all higher education degrees, policies that facilitate their participation in the labor force can have a large impact on the labor force participation rate and overall economic growth.

Another very successful policy tool to encourage labor force participation among low-income workers has been to raise the returns to work through the EITC, with the 1980s and 1990s EITC expansions pulling more than half a million people into the labor force. But the EITC available to workers without children and non-custodial parents (the "childless worker" EITC) is very small, and the current rules prevent workers younger than 25 and older than 64 from claiming the credit at all. The President has proposed to double the EITC available to workers without children and non-custodial parents and to make it available to younger and older workers. This policy would target a number of groups with falling or low labor force participation rates, including minority men, young adults not enrolled in school, workers with disabilities, and older workers.

In addition, to specifically support young men of color, the President launched the My Brother's Keeper Initiative in February 2014. This initiative created a Federal Task Force charged with assessing which public and private efforts are most effective at helping young men of color succeed academically, in their communities, and in the workplace. So far, eleven leading philanthropic foundations have committed to investing $200 million to study which programs keep these young men on track and bring these programs to scale.

Finally, building labor force attachment among young people can raise their labor force participation throughout life and offset the long-term declining trend. Earlier this year, the President announced $100 million in funding for American Apprenticeship Grants, which will use existing funds to expand apprenticeships, training young people for high-demand jobs, and helping them build relationships with employers. Additionally, the Administration will award $500 million to community colleges to implement job training programs based on the skills and credentials in demand among businesses. The President has similarly committed to redesigning high school curricula to focus more on industry-relevant skills. All of these initiatives aim to give young people labor market skills and connect them with employment opportunities, raising their labor force participation over the long-term.

The Cyclical Component of Participation

While the sections above highlight policies that can alter long-term labor force participation trends, a number of policies could noticeably reduce the cyclical drag on the participation rate by strengthening our economic recovery and increasing aggregate demand. For example, increasing investment in infrastructure would provide an immediate boost to employment and demand, as well as the long-term benefits of improved transportation systems. The President recently proposed a $302 billion four-year transportation reauthorization plan that would support hundreds of thousands of jobs.

Likewise, the President's proposal to increase investments in research, education, infrastructure, security, and other critical areas through the Budget's Opportunity, Growth, and Security Initiative would both speed the return to full employment and help lay the groundwork for stronger long-run growth. By strengthening the economy, this proposal could raise the cyclical portion of the labor force participation rate.

Extending Emergency Unemployment Compensation (EUC) would also boost economic activity and aggregate demand by supporting job-seekers' incomes while they are unemployed. Moreover, research shows that EUC helps long-term unemployed workers stay connected to the labor force and keep looking for work.

Other steps would also help, like reauthorizing the Export-Import Bank. In the absence of action from Congress, President Obama will press forward by using his executive authority to speed the permitting of infrastructure projects, launch new hubs of manufacturing innovation, and attract foreign investment.

The Administration is also taking action on its own to strengthen the recovery of the housing market. In May, the Federal Housing Administration (FHA) embarked on a program to address concerns about accessibility of mortgage credit, and acting independently, Federal Housing Finance Agency (FHFA) Director Mel Watt has also undertaken steps to provide clarity on so-called put-back risk and thereby ease credit constraints in the mortgage market. Also, the Administration has extended the Making Home Affordable program to continue to help struggling homeowners facing foreclosure or whose mortgages are underwater.

Factors Unique to the Great Recession: Long-term Unemployment

A complete recovery from the Great Recession will also require addressing the problem of long-term unemployment. Policies are needed to help the long-term unemployed find jobs and prevent them from leaving the labor force; the same policies may also help encourage some of those who have left the labor force over the last few years to re-enter it. One issue that researchers have identified is discrimination against the long-term unemployed by employers who often use computer programs or policies to screen out the long-term unemployed from job applicants. Long-term unemployed job seekers have to send out 3.5 times as many applications as short-term unemployed seekers to get an interview (Ghayad 2013). To address this and other issues facing the long-term unemployed, the President convened private sector leaders to discuss how the government and private industry can work together on this challenge.

More than 300 CEOs signed on to best practices for recruiting and hiring the long-term unemployed, including 80 of the nation's largest businesses and over 20 from the Fortune 50. The Administration is continuing to work with employers to learn and build on what works in helping the long-term unemployed return to work.

To further this cause, the Administration will use $150 million in existing funds to scale up partnerships between employers and non-profits that help get the long-term unemployed back to work through work-based training, job placement assistance, and employer outreach. The Administration also recognizes the value of extending EUC benefits in keeping the long-term unemployed workers attached to the labor force. Bringing down the rate of long-term unemployment through policies such as these, and strengthening the recovery overall, may help resolve the residual effect on labor force participation.

Appendix A. Time Series Analysis Specifications

Construction of a Cyclically-Adjusted Trend Component

A cyclically-adjusted trend component of the participation rate was estimated using a semiparametric procedure for a partially linear model (Robinson 1988, Stock 1989), combining a nonparametric biweight filter with a parametric cyclical adjustment step using leads and lags of the unemployment gap.

The biweight filter (using a window width of 40 quarters) was applied to the first difference of the participation rate and the trend component was constructed by cumulating the trend in first differences. First differences in the detrended participation were then regressed on two leads, two lags, and the present value of the unemployment gap.

The predicted values from this regression were cumulated to produce the estimated cyclical component, which was subtracted from the participation rate to adjust for the business cycle. The cyclically adjusted series was then run through the biweight filter in first differences again and the estimates were cumulated to produce the estimated trend component of the participation rate (Appendix Figure 3).

Looking at the period since the end of 2007, the estimated time series trend was very similar to the estimated aging effect, indicating that changes in participation within age groups may have offset and produced only a small reduction in total participation.

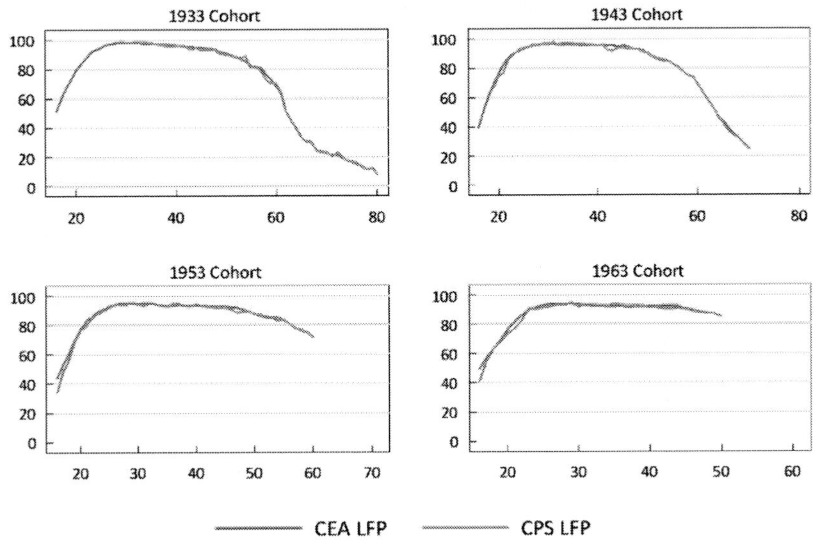

Appendix Figure 1. Male Participation Rates.

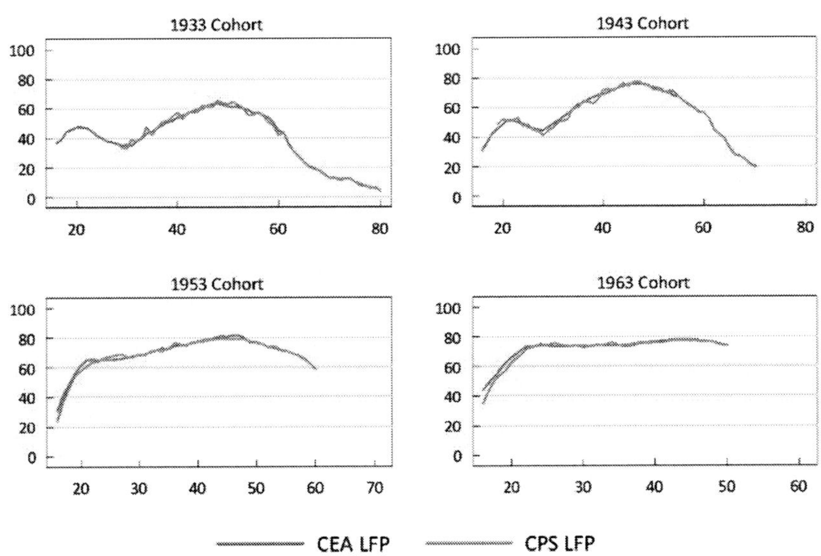

Appendix Figure 2. Female Participation Rates.

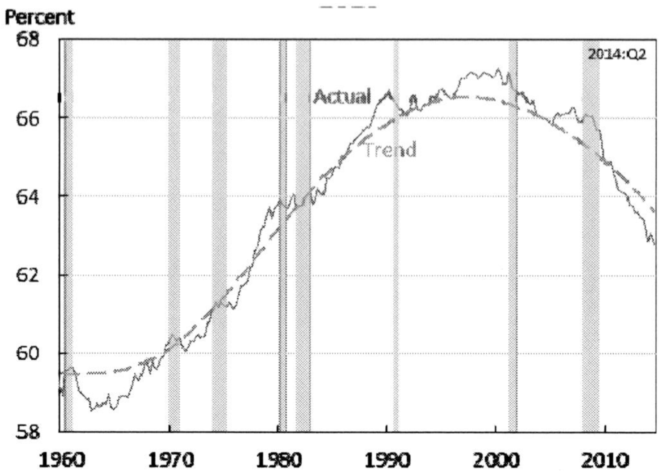

Appendix Figure 3. Estimated Time Series Trend, 1960-2013.

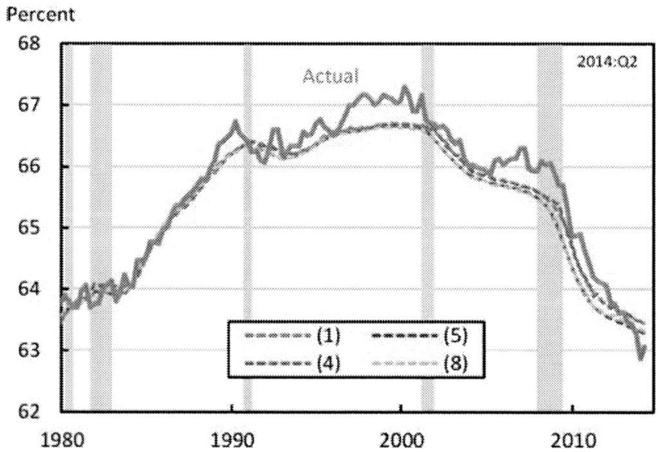

Appendix Figure 4. Estimated Cyclical Components from Regressions 1, 4, 5, and 8, 1980-2014.

References

Aaronson, Daniel, Jonathan Davis & Luojia Hu. (2012). "Explaining the Decline in the U.S. Labor Force Participation Rate." *Chicago Fed Letter*, 296.

Aaronson, Daniel, Kyung-Hong Park & Daniel Sullivan. (2006). "The Decline in Teen Labor Force Participation." *Economic Perspectives*, *Q1*, 2-18.

Aaronson, Stephanie, Bruce Fallick, Andrew Figura, Jonathan Pingle & William Wascher. (2006). "The Recent Decline in the Labor Force Participation Rate and Its Implications for Potential Labor Supply." *Brookings Papers on Economic Activity*, Spring, 69-154.

Abe, Masahiro, Yoshio Higuchi & Jane Waldfogel. (1998). "Maternity Leave Policies and Womens Employment after Childbirth: Evidence from the United States, Britain and Japan." Centre for Analysis of Social Exclusion, LSE.

Autor, David, H., David Dorn, & Gordon, H. Hanson. (2013). "Untangling Trade and Technology: Evidence from Local Labor Markets." Working Paper 18938. Cambridge, MA: National Bureau of Economic Research.

Autor, David & Duggan, Mark. 2003. "The Rise in the Disability Rolls and the Decline in Unemployment." *Quarterly Journal of Economics*, *118*(1), 157-206.

Autor, David, H., Lawrence, F. Katz & Melissa, S. Kearney. (2008). "Trends in U.S. Wage Inequality: Revising the Revisionists." *Review of Economics and Statistics.*

Bengali, Leila, Mary Daly & Rob Valletta. (2013). "Will Labor Force Participation Bounce Back?" Federal Reserve Bank of San Francisco Economic Letter, May 13.

Bertrand, Marianne & Sendhil Mullainathan. (2003). "Are Emily and Greg More Employable than Lakisha and Jamal? A Field Experiment on Labor Market Discrimination" Working Paper 9873. Cambridge, MA: National Bureau of Economic Research.

Blau, David, M. & Ryan, M. Goodstein. (2010). "Can Social Security Explain Trends in Labor Force Participation of Older Men in the United States?" *Journal of Human Resources*, *45*(2), 328-63.

Blau, Francine, D. & Lawrence, M. Kahn. (2013). "Female Labor Supply: Why is the US Falling Behind?" *Working Paper*, 7140. IZA Discussion Papers.

Borjas, George J., Jeffrey, Grogger & Gordon, H. Hanson. (2008). "Immigration and the Economic Status of African-American Men." *Economica*, *77*, 255–282.

Bound, John & Richard Freeman. (1992). "What Went Wrong? The Erosion of Relative Earnings and Employment among Young Black Men in the 1980s." *Quarterly Journal of Economics*, *108*, 201-32.

Bound, John, Michael Schauenbaum, & Timothy Waidmann. (1995). "Race and Education Differences in Disability Status and Labor Force Attachment in the Health and Retirement Survey," *Journal of Human Resources, 30* (Supplement 1995), S227-S267.

(BLS) Bureau of Labor Statistics. *Employment Projections – 2010-20.* US Department of Labor. February, *1.*

Casselman, Ben. "Missing: Up To 4 Million Workers." Fivethirtyeight.com. March 26, 2014.

Chandra, Amitabh. (2003). "Is the Convergence of the Racial Wage Gap Illusory?" Working Paper 9476. Cambridge, MA: National Bureau of Economic Research.

Coile, Courtney, C. (2004). "Retirement Incentives and Couples' Retirement Decisions." *Topics in Economic Analysis and Policy, 4*(1).

(CBO) Congressional Budget Office (2013). "The Economic Impact of S. 744, the Border Security, Economic Opportunity, and Immigration Modernization Act." *Congressional Budget Office.* June.

-- (2014). "The Slow Recovery of the Labor Market" *Congressional Budget Office.* February 2014.

Cowen, Tyler & Jayme Lemke. (2011). "10 Percent Unemployment Forever?" *Foreign Policy.* January 5.

Dahl, Gordon, B., Katrine, V. Løken, Magne Mogstad & Kari Vea Salvanes. (2013). "What Is the Case for Paid Maternity Leave?" Working Paper 19595. Cambridge, MA: National Bureau of Economic Research.

Danziger, Sheldon, & Gottschalk, Peter. (1995). *America Unequal.* New York: Russell Sage Foundation.

Elsby, Michael, Bart Hobijn, & Aysegül Sahin. (2013). "On the Importance of the Participation Margin for Labor Market Fluctuations." Unpublished manuscript.

Erceg, Christopher, J. & Andrew, T. Levin. (2013). "Labor Force Participation and Monetary Policy in the Wake of the Great Recession." *Federal Reserve Bank of Boston,* April.

Fallick, Bruce & Jonathan Pingle. (2007). "A Cohort-Based Model of Labor Force Participation." Board of Governors of the Federal Reserve System, Finance and Economics Discussion Series Working Paper, 2007-09.

--. 2013. Data update to "A Cohort-Based Model of Labor Force Participation." September, 2013.

Fairlie, Robert W., Kanika Kapur, & Susan Gates. (2011). "Is Employer-based Health Insurance a Barrier to Entrepreneurship?" *Journal of Health Economics, 30*(1), 146-162.

Fernandez, Raquel. (2013). "Cultural Change as Learning: The Evolution of Female Labor Force Participation over a Century" *American Economic Review*, *103*(1), 472-500.

Fogg, Neeta P. & Paul E. Harrington. (2011). "The Collapse of the Labor Market for 16-24 Year-Olds." *Cascade: No. 78.* Fall 2011.

Freeman, Richard, B. (2003). "Can We Close the Revolving Door?: Recidivism vs Employment of Ex-Offenders in the U.S." *Urban Institute Reentry Roundtable.* May 19-20, 2003.

Fujita, Shigeru. (2014). "On the Causes of Declines in the Labor Force Participation Rate." *Federal* Reserve *Bank of Philadelphia. February, 6.*

Ghayad, Rand. (2013). "The Jobless Trap." Working Paper.

Goldin, Claudia & Lawrence F. Katz. (1998). "The Origins of Technology-Skill Complementarity*." The Quarterly Journal of Economics*, *113*(3), 693-732.

--. (2007). "Long-run changes in the US wage structure: narrowing, widening, polarizing." Working Paper 13568. Cambridge, MA: National Bureau of Economic Research.

Gustman, Alan L. & Thomas, Steinmeier. (2008). "How Changes in Social Security Affect Recent Retirement Trends." Working Paper 14105. Cambridge, MA: National Bureau of Economic Research.

Gustman, Alan, L., Thomas, L. Steinmeier & Nahid Tabatabai. (2011). "How Did the Recession of 2007-2009 Affect the Wealth and Retirement of the Near Retirement Age Population in the Health and Retirement Study?" Working Paper 17547. Cambridge, MA: National Bureau of Economic Research.

Holzer, Harry J., Paul Offner & Elaine Sorrenson. (2005). "Declining Employment Among Young Black Less-Educated Men: The Role of Incarceration and Child Support." *Journal of Policy Analysis and Management*, *24*(2), 329-350.

Holzer, Harry J., Steven Raphael, & Michael A. Stoll. (2006). "Perceived Criminality, Criminal Background Checks, and the Racial Hiring Practices of Employers." *Journal of Law and Economics"*, *49*(2), 451-480.

--. (2002). "How do Crime and Incarceration Affect the Employment Prospects of Less-educated Young Black Men?" *Extending Opportunity Conference.* Washington DC: May 2002.

Juhn, Chinhui. (1992). "The Decline in Male Labor Market Participation: The Role of Declining Market Opportunities," *Quarterly Journal of Economics*, *107*(1), 79-121.

--. (2003). "Labor Market Dropouts and Trends in the Wages of Black and White Men," *Industrial and Labor Relations Review*, *56*, 643-662.

Kahn, Lisa B. (2010). "The Long-term Labor Market Consequences of Graduating from College in a Bad Economy." *Labour Economics*, *17*(2), 303-316.

Karoly, Lynn, A. & Julie Zissimopoulos. (2004)"Self-Employment among Older U.S. Workers." *Monthly Labor Review*, *27*(7), 24-47.

Kroft, Kory, Fabian Lange, & Matthew, J. Notowidigdo. (2013). "Duration Dependence and Labor Market Conditions: Evidence from a Field Experiment." *The Quarterly Journal of Economics.*, *128*(3), 1123-1167.

Kroft, Kory, Fabian Lange, & Matthew J. Notowidigdo & Lawrence, F. Katz. (2014). "Long-Term Unemployment and the Great Recession: The Role of Composition, Duration Dependence, and Non-Participation." Working Paper 20273. Cambridge, MA: National Bureau of Economic Research.

Krueger, Alan B., Judd Cramer & David Cho. (2014). "Are the Long-Term Unemployed on the Margins of the Labor Market?" Working Paper. Washington, DC: Brookings Panel on Economic Activity. March, *10*.

Kudlyak, Marianna. (2013). "A Cohort Model of Labor Force Participation." *Economic Quarterly*, *99*(1), 25-43. First Quarter 2013.

Maestas, Nicole & Julie Zissimopoulos. (2010). "How Longer Work Lives Ease the Crunch of Population Aging." *Journal of Economic Perspectives*, *24*(1), 139-160.

Maestas, Nicole. (2007). "Back to Work: Expectations and Realizations of Work after Retirement." *Journal of Human Resources*, 45(3), 718-748.

Mitchell, Josh. 2013. "Who are the long-term unemployed?" Washington, DC: The Urban Institute. July.

Moynihan, Daniel, P. (1965). "Employment, Income, and the Ordeal of the Negro Family." Daedalus, *9*(4), The Negro American. Fall 1965.

Pager, Deyah. (2003). "The Mark of a Criminal Record." *American Journal of Sociology*, *108*(5), 937-975.

Pattison, David & Hilary Waldron. (2013). "Growth in New Disabled-Worker Entitlements, 1970–2008." Social Security Bulletin. 73(4).

Reed, Deborah & Sheldon Danziger. 2007. "The Effects of Recent Immigration on Racial/Ethnic Labor Market Differentials." *American Economic Review*, 97(2), 373-77.

Robinson P. M. (1988). "Root-N-consistent Semiparametric Regression." *Econometrica*, *56*, 931-954.

Rossin-Slater, Maya, Christopher J. Ruhm & Jane Waldfogel. (2013). "The Effects of California's Paid Family Leave Program on Mothers' Leave-

Taking and Subsequent Labor Market Outcomes," *Journal of Policy Analysis and Management*, *32*(2), 224-245,

Schirle, Tammy. (2008). "Why Have the Labor Force Participation Rates of Older Men Increased since the Mid-1990s?" *Journal of Labor Economics*, *26*(4), 549-594.

Shierholz, Heidi. (2012). "Labor Force Participation: Cyclical versus Structural Changes since the Start of the Great Recession." *Economic Policy Institute*. Issue Brief #333. May 24, 2012.

Smith, Christopher. (2008). "Dude, Where's My Job? The Impact of Immigration on the Youth Labor Market." Unpublished Ph.D. dissertation, Department of Economics, Massachusetts Institute of Technology.

--. (2011). Polarization, Immigration, Education: What's Behind the Dramatic Decline in Youth Employment? Division of Research and Statistics and Monetary Affairs, Federal Reserve Board.

Stock, James H. (1989). "Nonparametric Policy Analysis." *Journal of the American Statistical Association*, *84*(406), 567-575.

Travis, J., Amy L. Solomon & Michelle, Waul. (2001). *From Prison to Home: The Dimensions and Consequences of Prisoner Reentry*. Washington DC: Urban Institute Press.

Van Zandweghe, Willem. (2012). "Interpreting the Recent Decline in Labor Force Participation," *Federal Reserve Bank of Kansas City Economic Review*, First Quarter 2012, 5-34.

Western, Bruce & Becky Pettit. (2000). "Incarceration and Racial Inequality in Men's Employment." *Industrial and Labor Relations Review*, *54*(1), 3-16.

In: The Labor Force Participation Rate
Editor: Darrel Graves

ISBN: 978-1-63463-391-8

Chapter 2

RETURNING TO FULL EMPLOYMENT: WHAT DO THE INDICATORS TELL US?*

Marc Labonte

SUMMARY

Until recently, the economy and labor market were experiencing an unusually slow recovery from the longest and deepest recession since the Great Depression compared to other expansions since World War II. The rapid decline in the unemployment rate from 7.9% in January to 6.7% in December 2013 (where it remained in the first quarter of 2014) would seem to indicate that the labor market is returning to normal. The current unemployment rate is only 0.5 to 1.5 percentage points higher than the consensus range of full employment.

Unusually, the unemployment rate may not currently be a good proxy for the overall state of the labor market or economy. Some of the decline in the unemployment rate in 2013 is attributable to a recovery in employment, but some is attributable to workers dropping out of the labor force. The labor force participation rate has continued to fall during the recovery and is at its lowest level since the 1970s. In fact, it has fallen more in the past five years than at any time since data have been collected. Studies have identified multiple reasons for the decline. Some workers have left the labor force because they have become discouraged

* This is an edited, reformatted and augmented version of a Congressional Research Service publication R43476, prepared for Members and Committees of Congress, dated April 15, 2014.

and given up on seeking employment. Others have left for reasons stemming from long-term trends that are unrelated to the recession, such as age or enrollment in school or training. This trend could reverse—for example, more workers returned to the labor force than found jobs in the first quarter of 2014, which prevented the unemployment rate from falling.

Other evidence also points to more slack in the economy than the headline unemployment rate suggests. Economic output and employment have grown since mid-2009 and 2010, respectively, but at relatively sluggish rates. The long-term unemployment rate and youth unemployment rates have fallen only modestly since the recession ended and are still at historically high levels. Inflation has remained slightly lower than the Federal Reserve's (Fed's) goal of 2%.

These other economic indicators could be sending a misleading signal about significant slack in the economy, however, if the economy's potential capacity has been eroded by structural changes or by the length and depth of the Great Recession. Cyclical deterioration in the U.S. labor market is usually considered temporary—recessions are thought to have no lasting effect on overall employment and unemployment rates. This recession could cause a departure from conventional wisdom if labor market problems that started as cyclical persisted so long that they became structural. For example, long-term unemployment could have caused workers' skills to erode, which would then prevent them from finding a job when the economy recovered.

Congress conducts fiscal policy and oversees the Fed's implementation of monetary policy, the two tools of macroeconomic stabilization. Policy makers are grappling with the transition from the highly expansionary monetary and fiscal policy put in place during the Great Recession. Many economists advocate reducing the budget deficit only when the economy is at or near full employment. Likewise, the Fed has stated that it would begin to raise interest rates once the economy is near full employment. If the economy remains far from full employment, then declining unemployment would not yet call for a tightening of monetary and fiscal policy. Alternatively, if lower unemployment is being driven by a cyclical upswing and the economy is now closer to full employment than historical experience would predict, policy would likely need to be tightened sooner in order to avoid rising inflation. It would also suggest that structural policies (e.g., those that increase the incentives to hire, seek work, delay retirement, or train) would be more effective at improving labor market conditions than counter-cyclical monetary and fiscal policies.

The unemployment rate declined markedly in 2013, to 6.7% in December from 7.9% in January, seeming to signal that the labor market is approaching full employment. Other economic and labor market indicators paint a more pessimistic picture, however. For example, the decline in the unemployment rate was caused in part by workers dropping out of the labor force. The labor force participation rate has fallen to under 63% at the end of 2013 from 66% before the recession. Understanding this divergence is crucial for an accurate assessment of the current state of the economic recovery and of how close the economy is to full employment.

This report analyzes recent trends in labor market indicators during the current economic recovery, with a particular focus on the contrast between the unemployment rate and other labor market indicators.[1] It reviews studies that have sought to determine how much of the decline in the labor force participation rate is caused by the recession and how much is caused by structural factors, such as the aging of the labor force. It then considers whether the economy might reach full employment at a higher rate of unemployment compared to recent expansions.[2] It concludes by analyzing the implications of these developments for macroeconomic stabilization policy, as policy makers grapple with the transition from the expansionary fiscal and monetary policy put in place during the "Great Recession." If the labor market has experienced structural changes, it would also have implications for labor market and other microeconomic policies (e.g., spending or tax provisions that increase the incentives to hire, seek work, delay retirement, or train), which are beyond the scope of this report.

Labor Market Conditions During the Great Recession and Current Recovery

Contraction and Recovery in the Labor Market as Measured by Unemployment and Employment

The most recent recession, often referred to as the Great Recession, caused the unemployment rate to rise to 10.0% in October 2009 from 4.4% in May 2007.[3] That increase was the largest since the Great Depression, and only the second time that unemployment has reached double digits since the Great Depression.[4] The recession caused the economy to move far below full employment. Full employment is the concept that all of the economy's labor and capital resources are in use—there is little idle capacity and unemployment is at its natural rate (defined in the text box below). At its peak, the unemployment rate was 4.3 percentage points above the Congressional Budget Office's (CBO's) estimate of the natural rate of unemployment, the second highest level reached since 1949.[5] The number of workers employed fell by 8.7 million during and after the recession, from a peak of 138.4 million in January 2008 to a low of 129.7 million in February 2010.

What Is the Natural Rate of Unemployment?

The unemployment rate follows a predictable cyclical pattern—it trends down when the economy is growing, and it trends up when the economy is in recession. It never reaches zero, however, as there will always be some people moving between jobs at any given time, even when the economy is booming. This has led economists to posit that there is a *natural rate of unemployment* that the economy gravitates to when the economy is at full employment. At any point in time, the actual unemployment rate consists of a cyclical component and the underlying natural rate. The unemployment rate may briefly decline below the natural rate, but economic theory predicts that this will trigger rising inflation, as it is indicative of an overheating economy.[6]

Because the natural rate of unemployment is a theoretical construct, it cannot be observed directly and must be inferred. Different economists have different estimates, but the consensus falls within a relatively narrow range. For example, the Federal Reserve governors and regional bank presidents estimate a natural rate of 5.2% to 6.0%.[7] CBO estimates that the natural rate has currently been elevated to 6.0%, but will eventually return to 5.5%.[8] In the FY2015 President's budget, the Office of Management and Budget projected an unemployment rate of 5.4% in the out years of the budget window. (By comparison, the *actual* unemployment rate ranged from 4.4% to 4.7% at the end of the previous economic expansion.) The natural rate may vary over time, and the question of whether it has recently risen is discussed in the section below entitled "A Rising Natural Rate of Unemployment?"

For background on the natural rate, see CRS Report RL30391, *Inflation and Unemployment: What is the Connection?*, by Brian W. Cashell.

The unusually deep recession has been followed by an unusually slow recovery. Although the recession officially ended in June 2009, the *unemployment rate* continued to rise until October 2009, and showed no marked decline until the second quarter of 2010. It has fallen in spurts since. Overall, the unemployment rate has fallen more gradually than in other recoveries since World War II. After 18 quarters of recovery and counting, the unemployment rate is still above what most economists believe to be the natural rate of unemployment. Only the 1980s recovery faced a comparably long return to full employment, nearing full employment after 19 quarters.[9] And, because the unemployment rate was so high at its peak in the Great Recession and has fallen slowly, it has been at historically high levels for most of the recovery. In 2012, three years into the recovery, it averaged 8.1%, which was a higher unemployment rate than experienced during all except the two deepest recessions between 1948 and 2001.

Another method to gauge the pace of labor market improvement is to count the number of months until *total employment* returned to its pre-recession peak level. In every recession since World War II through the 1990s, employment surpassed its previous peak in less than a year and a half. After the 2001 recession, it took over three years. After six years, employment today has still not returned to its peak level in January 2008 of 138.4 million workers. Since the non-elderly adult population is expanding by over one million each year, in order to return to full employment, the number of people employed should not only return to its former peak, but surpass it. One study put the economy at 10 million jobs short of full employment in mid-2009.[10] CBO estimated that the economy was still 6 million jobs short of full employment at the end of 2013.[11]

Employment has not returned to its peak because the decline in employment during the recession was so great, and because the rate of employment growth during the recovery has been relatively tepid compared to other recoveries, particularly those that followed deep recessions. *Figure 1* shows that the average monthly job loss was much greater from 2008 to 2010 than in the three preceding episodes (1982, 1991, 2002 to 2003), where recessions caused employment to fall. It also shows that average monthly job growth in this recovery was much lower than in the 1980s or 1990s expansions, and comparable to the 2000s expansion, even though far fewer jobs were lost in 2002 and 2003.

The *unemployment rate* fell relatively rapidly in 2013, to 6.7% in December from 7.9% in January. It has remained around that level in the first quarter of 2014. If the natural rate of unemployment is between 5.2% and 6.0%, then unemployment moved from well above the natural rate at the beginning of 2013 to within about a half of a percentage point of the high end of the estimated range by the end of 2013.[12]

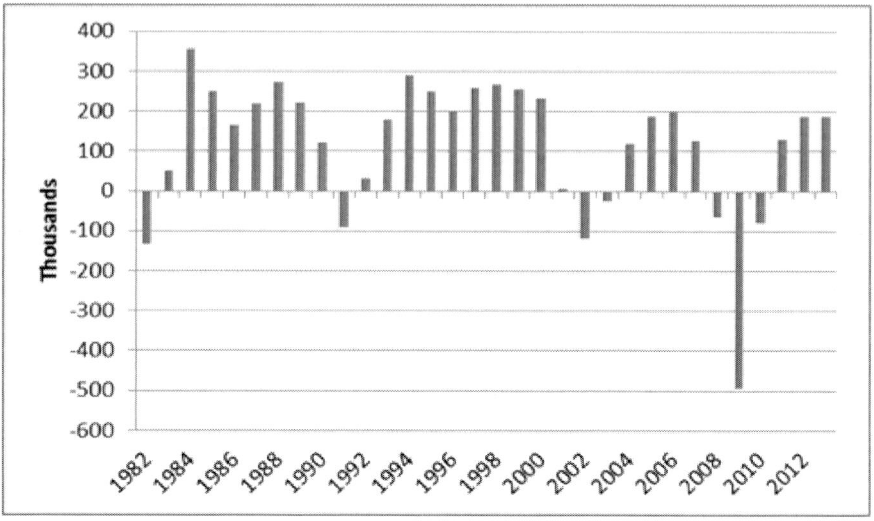

Source: Bureau of Labor Statistics, Current Employment Statistics.

Figure 1. Average Monthly Employment Growth. (1982 to 2013)

The relatively rapid decline in the unemployment rate in 2013 was not matched by consistently rapid *job growth*, however. (For an explanation of how these data are measured, see the following text box.) The number of unemployed workers declined by a monthly average of 160,000 per month in 2013. According to CPS data, job growth averaged 115,000 per month in 2013, lower than in 2011 or 2012.[13] Unemployment declined faster than employment grew in 2013 because an average of 45,000 workers exited the labor force each month. In normal economic expansions, the labor force grows along with the population.

How Are Unemployment and Employment Measured?

The Bureau of Labor Statistics has two separate measures of employment. The Current Employment Statistics survey (CES, "payroll survey") measures employment based on a survey of employers, and the Current Population Survey (CPS, "household survey") measures employment based on a survey of households. Both measures are official, but the Current Employment Statistics survey is generally the preferred source of data on employment because it has the larger, more robust sample. There are some definitional differences between the two surveys.

For example, the CPS includes the self-employed, but the CES does not. For the CES, workers are considered employed if they are "on establishment payrolls employed full- or part-time who received pay (whether they worked or not) for any part of the pay period that includes the 12th day of the month."

Unemployment and other labor force measures can only be measured through the CPS, however—the CES, based on payroll records, provides no information on the unemployed or those who have left the labor force. As a result, discussions of what is driving the unemployment rate can only be based on the CPS, although this is not the preferred source of employment data. Workers are considered unemployed "if they do not have a job, have actively looked for work in the prior 4 weeks, and are currently available for work." The labor force consists of employed and unemployed workers. If workers would like a job, but are not actively seeking employment, they are not counted as unemployed; rather, they are considered out of the labor force. Labor force data are typically reported for the population 16 years and older. The unemployment rate is expressed as a percentage of the labor force, not the population.

Because the two surveys use different samples and concepts, they report different rates of job growth on a month-tomonth basis. These differences tend to average out over longer periods of time. In 2013, employment increased by 2.3 million according to the CES and by 1.5 million according to the CPS.

Source: Bureau of Labor Statistics, Frequently Asked Questions, http://www.bls.gov/ces/cesfaq.htm and http://www.bls.gov/cps/faq.htm.

Any interpretation of the current health of the economic recovery must explain why 45,000 workers left the labor force each month in 2013, and why over 3% of the population has left the labor force since 2008, as shown in *Figure 2*—the topic of the next section.

The Labor Force Participation Rate Has Continued to Fall During the Recovery

The labor force participation rate (LFPR) is the share of the population that is employed or unemployed. As can be seen in *Figure 2,* the LFPR hovered around 59% from after World War II to the late 1960s. It then experienced a long upward trend primarily because of the increased participation of women in the labor force, peaking at 67% in the late 1990s. Following the 2001 recession, it fell to 66%, where it remained until the Great Recession began.[14] Since 2008, it has continued to fall, and stood at 62.8% at the end of 2013.

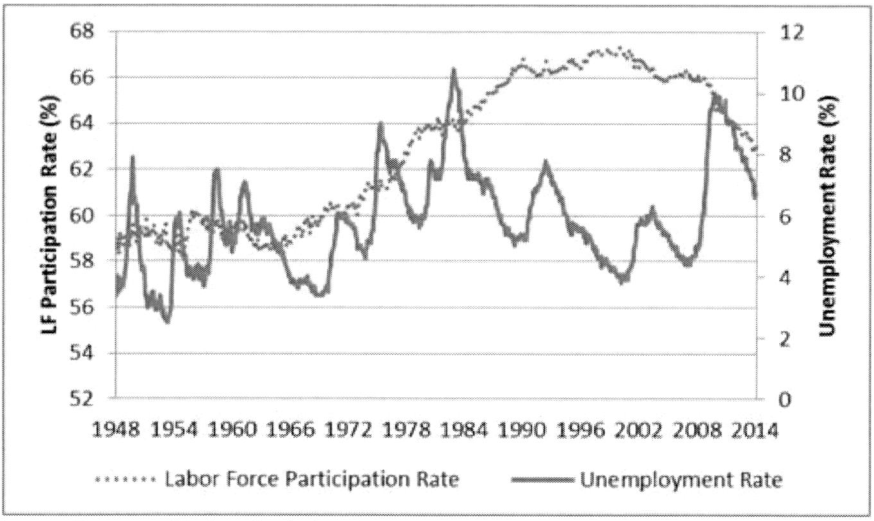

Source: Bureau of Labor Statistics, Current Population Survey.

Figure 2. Unemployment and Labor Force Participation. (1948 to 2014).

This decline is unprecedented. Since World War II, the participation rate has never before fallen significantly in an expansion and has exhibited only modest cyclicality[15]—it declined by less than one percentage point during the 1980, 1991-1992, and 2001 recessions, and did not decline in the others. (If all workers who lost their jobs in a recession became unemployed (according to the official definition), the labor force participation rate would not change, all else being equal.) According to one study: "In the four years [2007-2011] since the start of the recent recession, the LFPR has declined faster than in any preceding four-year period on record."[16]

While the long-term upward trend in the LFPR until 2000 was dominated by the entry of women into the work force, the recent recession caused both male and female participation to decline. The female participation rate experienced a nearly uninterrupted ascent to 60.0% in 2000 from 32.7% in 1948. Since, it has fallen to 57.2% in 2013 from 59.5% in 2008. By contrast, the longterm trend in the male participation rate has been downward in the post-war period, falling to 73.0% in 2008 from 86.6% in 1948. The decline has been particularly rapid since 2008, however, falling to 69.7% in 2013—the lowest level ever recorded.

Viewed by age cohort, the LFPR decline has been concentrated among prime age adults (age 25 to 54) and particularly among youth (age 16 to 24), whose participation rate has fallen by more than ten percentage points since 2000.[17] By contrast, the participation rate of older workers (age 55 and older) rose from the late 1990s through 2009, the last year of the recession; it has since levelled off. There are different theories as to why the participation rate of older workers would be higher than before the recession while it fell for other age cohorts. One hypothesis is that older workers have postponed retirement because of the decline in wealth caused by the housing and financial crises.[18] Another hypothesis is that the LFPR of older workers has not fallen because the cohort of women recently turning age 55 has a much higher labor force participation rate than earlier cohorts of women when they turned age 55; however, the LFPR for older men has also risen.[19]

The implications of the decline in the LFPR for an assessment of the health of the economic recovery depend on why workers are leaving the labor force. Workers can leave for various reasons, including retirement, injury or illness, family reasons, study or training, or because they have become discouraged and stopped looking for a job. As noted above, once workers stop looking for a job, they are no longer officially counted as unemployed.

Why did the LFPR fall so much during the recession and why is it still falling in the recovery? It could be cyclical, caused by the Great Recession, or it could be structural, caused by long-term forces unrelated to the recession. If the latter, these structural factors would reduce growth in the economy's potential output, rather than be a symptom of weak economic growth.

Several recent studies (which are compared in *Table 1*) have attempted to identify the causes of the decline in the participation rate.[20] All studies found that the decline has been caused by both structural and cyclical factors, although the relative importance of the two factors varied across studies. All of these studies agree that the aging of the population is a structural factor behind the recent decline—as more "baby boomers" move out of the prime working age cohorts, into older cohorts, they are retiring.[21] Another cause of a declining LFPR has been an increase in workers claiming disability, who tend to be older workers.[22] Some studies also identified higher rates of school enrollment as another cause of the decline in the participation rate.[23] But the studies found that these factors cannot account for the entire drop in the participation rate, and the studies attribute the rest of the decline to cyclical factors.[24] The increase in workers classified by BLS as discouraged or marginally attached to the labor force, from about 1% of the labor force before the recession to 1.5% of the labor force since, is further evidence that some of the recent decline in the participation rate is cyclical.[25]

Table 1. Studies Explaining the Decline in the Labor Force Participation Rate

Study	Period Covered	Cyclical or Structural?	Methods	Notes
Erceg/Levin	2007 to early 2013	25% of 2.5 pp overall decline is structural, 75% is cyclical; 100% of 2 pp decline is cyclical for ages 25-54.	state level data; reweighting of age cohorts	
CBO	end of 2007 to end of 2013	1.5 pp due to structural trends, 1 pp cyclical and temporary, 0.5 pp caused by recession and permanent.	not available	Structural is attributed primarily to aging of population; increased disability claimants and early retirements are classified as caused by recession and permanent.
Aaronson et al.	2000 to end of 2011	1.2 pp decline structural, 1.5 pp other.	demographic microdata	Age 16 to 79. "Other" could be cyclical; of structural, 0.8 pp chg in age distribution, 0.4 pp chg in gender share or educational attainment.
Aaronson et al.	2008 to end of 2011	25% of 1.8 pp decline is structural, 75% other.	demographic microdata	Age 16 to 79. "Other" could be cyclical.
Hotchkiss et al.	2008 to end of 2011	Increase in "Schooling" and "Other" as reasons given for leaving LF for age 25-54 and increase in	questionnaire on reasons for leaving LF	Questionnaire includes discouraged workers in "Other" category. Authors believe that "Schooling" and

Study	Period Covered	Cyclical or Structural?	Methods	Notes
		"Other" category for age 16 to 24.		"Other" categories are most likely to re-enter LF in the future. No change in trend for age 55 and older.
Van Zandweghe	Dec. 2007 to Dec. 2011	A = half of 2 pp decline is attributable to shift in age distribution; B = 1.1 pp due to cyclical downturn, 0.8 pp due to long-term trends.	A= demographic data; B = trend-cycle (Beveridge-Nelson) decomposition	Two methods are used to derive two separate estimates (A and B).
Sherk	2007 to 2012	A = of 2.3 pp decline, reason for leaving was 0.8 pp retirement, 0.7 pp disability, 0.9 pp school, -0.2 pp family; B = demographic adjustment explains 0.6 pp; of remaining 1.7 pp, -0.6 pp retirement, 0.9 pp disability, 1.1 pp school, 0.1 pp other	questionnaire on reasons for leaving LF; demographic data	Two methods are used: A = questionnaire with no demographic adjustment; B = questionnaire with demographic adjustment. Retirement becomes negative after demographic adjustment b/c retirement rate has not gone up among older workers.
Morgan Stanley	Dec. 2007 to Dec. 2013	Of 3.2 pp decline, 2.0 pp is demographic, 0.3 pp is disability, 0.4 pp is school enrollment, and 0.5 is other discouraged (residual).	demographic data; data on disability and school enrollment	Authors label disability as structural (permanent); schooling and other LF dropouts as cyclical (temporary).

While these studies have categorized reasons for leaving the labor force as either cyclical or structural, both reasons can cause a person to leave the labor force. Cyclical considerations are sometimes a contributing factor to an individual's decision to leave the labor force for reasons assumed to be structural (retirement, disability,[26] or school enrollment)—when job prospects are poor, the alternatives to working become relatively more attractive. For example, if a worker returned to school to switch careers, this could be considered structural, but if a worker returned to school because there was temporarily no work available, this could be considered cyclical.

Although the LFPR has not been cyclical in the past, that does not rule out a cyclical decline since 2007 due to the unusual severity of the recent recession and the weakness of the recovery. If some of the decline in the participation rate is cyclical, that portion would be expected to be reversed in the coming years. Counterintuitively, an improving recovery could potentially result in a higher unemployment rate if workers return to the labor force faster than positions are created or filled. This explains why the unemployment rate did not fall in the first quarter of 2014—more people entered the labor force than gained employment, leading to an increase in the number of people unemployed.[27]

Workers who take early retirement or claim disability benefits are characterized across studies as likely to remain outside the labor force permanently.[28] CBO attributes 0.5 percentage points of the decline to people who left the labor force because of the recession and are unlikely to return.[29] A challenge for policy makers is to encourage and support the re-entry into the labor force of workers who left involuntarily (e.g., because they lost their job) as the job market strengthens.

The Labor Market Experience of Selected Groups

Recovery in the labor market has been uneven. Some groups have lower employment and higher unemployment rates than the overall labor force, and these groups have experienced a weaker rebound during the economic recovery than the overall labor force. Their experience points to areas of continued labor market weakness that are masked by the improvement in the overall unemployment rate.

Long-Term Unemployment

The percentage of workers who are unemployed long-term (defined by BLS as 27 weeks or more) rose to 4.3% of all workers in the second quarter of 2010 from 0.8% in 2007—the highest rate recorded since data were first collected in 1948. It then fell to 2.6% at the end of 2013; despite the decline, it remained higher than at any point from 1948 to 2008.[30] In 2013, the percentage of unemployed workers who were unemployed long-term was 37.6%, up from 17.6% in 2007 and higher than at any time before 2008. The long-term unemployed are less likely to find work and more likely to leave the labor force than the short-term unemployed; this difference in outcomes is greater during an expansion.[31]

Youth Employment and Unemployment

The Great Recession hit the young particularly hard. In 2010, employment rates were the lowest (45.0%) and unemployment rates were the highest (18.4%) on record for the 16 to 24 age group, with data going back to 1948.[32] Since then, the youth employment rate has improved only modestly—in contrast to previous recoveries—to 47.4% at the end of 2013; it remains lower than in any year between 1948 and 2008. The youth unemployment rate declined significantly in 2013, to 13.5% at the end of 2013, before increasing to 14.4% in February 2014. It nevertheless remains at a historically high level.

As discussed above, the youth labor force participation rate has not increased since the recession ended. According to one study, the most frequent reason given by youth for leaving the labor force was education/training, but that reason did not increase in relative frequency during the recession. The only category of reason for leaving the labor force that increased during that period was the "other" category, that is, people who did not give one of the survey's pre-identified reasons for leaving. The authors believe that individuals who gave these two reasons for leaving the labor force were most likely to re-enter in the future.[33]

Alternative Measurements of Labor Underutilization

The Bureau of Labor Statistics compiles six measures of labor underutilization based on varying categories of work status, one of which is the official unemployment rate (technically, it is referred to as the U-3). Two of these measures include fewer workers than the official unemployment rate and three include more. The broadest BLS measure of labor underutilization is called the U-6 measure, and it includes the unemployed, persons marginally attached to the labor force, and those employed part-time for economic reasons. Workers employed part-time for economic reasons account for most of the difference between the U-6 and U-3 historically. All of these measures follow a similar pattern—a sharp increase during the recession, followed by a slow and modest decline during the recovery. For example, U-6 peaked at

17.1% in the fourth quarter of 2009, and then fell to 13.3% in fourth quarter of 2013, which is higher than at any point from 1994 to before the financial crisis. According to the president of the Boston Fed:

> While there is always a difference between U-3 and U-6, as there are always some marginally attached and part-time workers in the economy, the spread between the U-3 and U-6 measures of unemployment has increased dramatically since the start of the financial crisis.[34]

A high U-6 rate does not imply that the economy will not reach full employment until the U-6 declines to the natural rate. Conceptually, just as the actual U-6 is always higher than the actual U-3 (headline) unemployment rate, a natural rate for U-6 could be estimated that would be higher than the natural rate for U-3. The drawback to using U-6 data to measure the relative slack in the economy is that data go back only to 1994, so there is data covering only the last two recessions. This makes it difficult to ascertain whether the U-6 or U-3 is currently providing more accurate information on the state of the economy.

A Rising Natural Rate of Unemployment?

The slow decline in the unemployment rate and continued lack of employment opportunities for youth and the long-term unemployed in the current recovery have raised concerns that the natural rate of unemployment may have risen recently. In other words, there is a concern that when the economy returns to full employment, it will be at a higher unemployment rate than that obtained in prior expansions.

Since the natural rate is defined as the underlying rate of unemployment once cyclical factors are removed, conventional economic theory posits that changes in the natural rate would be driven only by structural factors unrelated to the business cycle, such as demographics. An alternative theory that economists are now considering is that the natural rate of unemployment has permanently increased as a result of the depth and duration of the Great Recession and subsequent jobless recovery, and not because of any long-term structural causes.[35] Economists refer to this concept as “hysteresis.” One reason that hysteresis might occur is because workers’ skills erode during bouts of long-term unemployment, making them less employable going forward.[36]

Reaching a consensus on whether the protracted period of high unemployment was the result of temporarily inadequate aggregate demand, an upward shift in the natural rate of unemployment unrelated to the recession, or an upward shift caused by hysteresis will require more evidence— notably, how much further unemployment falls in the current expansion before inflation rises. In the past, there has been little evidence of hysteresis in the United States, but the phenomenon has been observed in parts of Europe.[37] That does not preclude hysteresis in this case, however, given the unusual depth and duration of the Great Recession and subsequent tepid recovery.

CBO has estimated that the natural rate of unemployment rose to 6% in 2013 from 5% in 2007.[38] CBO attributed 0.5 percentage points of the increase to "the stigma of long-term unemployment," 0.5 percentage points to "a decrease in the efficiency with which employers filled vacancies," and 0.1 percentage points to "the incentives generated in 2013 by extensions of unemployment insurance benefits." CBO attributed the decrease in the efficiency of filling vacancies at least in part to mismatches between skills and openings, and expects the increase in the natural rate attributable to it to be temporary.[39]

Changes in the natural rate are not uncommon historically. For example, economists believe that it rose in the 1970s and fell in the 1990s. Estimated variations in the natural rate over time are typically modest, however. CBO has estimated that it has ranged from 5.0% to 6.3% since 1949.[40]

Evidence for and against a rise in the natural rate is presented in CRS Report, *The Increase in Unemployment Since 2007: Is It Cyclical or Structural?* If the natural rate has increased, it would mean that the economy is closer to full employment today than estimates based on the natural rate prevailing before the recession would suggest. If so, there are macroeconomic policy implications, which are discussed in the next section.

MACROECONOMIC POLICY IMPLICATIONS

Historically, the headline unemployment rate has been viewed as a simple, timely, and transparent indicator of the state of the economy. There are several other indicators of slack in the economy and the labor market, but, as long as those measures are relatively well correlated with the headline unemployment rate, as they typically are, the unemployment rate provides a simple ruleof-thumb gauge of how close the economy is to full employment.[41]

Until recently, the economy was unambiguously operating far below full employment. By the end of 2013, the unemployment rate was coming within a percentage point of the mainstream range of the natural rate of unemployment. Were the recent pace of improvement in the unemployment rate to continue, unemployment could fall to the natural rate in the next year or two.

As this report has discussed, other indicators have diverged from the unemployment rate and suggest that significant slack remains in the economy. These include labor market indicators (e.g., modest employment growth and flat wages) and other indicators (e.g., the large output gap[42] and the low inflation rate). While most measures show the economy modestly improving since the recession ended, the labor force participation rate has continued to deteriorate over the course of the recovery. Studies have concluded that the participation rate has fallen partly for cyclical reasons and partly for structural reasons.

Most economists believe the primary goal of short-term macroeconomic stabilization policy is to bring the economy back to full employment in a timely fashion and keep it there, while maintaining price stability. They believe "counter-cyclical" policy, which boosts growth when the economy is distressed and reins in growth when it is overheating, can be used to blunt the extremes of the business cycle. While there is consensus that policy can hypothetically achieve this goal, there is disagreement on the likelihood that appropriate policies will be chosen in reality, and whether the policies that are likely to be chosen could make matters worse.

Policy makers have two macroeconomic stabilization tools, fiscal policy and monetary policy, at their disposal. Congress is directly responsible for fiscal policy through its control of federal revenue and spending provisions. Congress has delegated the operation of monetary policy to the Federal Reserve, but exercises oversight.

In the mainstream economic view, Congress can hasten economic recovery by increasing the budget deficit (fiscal stimulus).[43] But borrowing has long-term economic costs and inter-generational equity implications, and the benefits of fiscal stimulus decline as the economy approaches full employment. Thus, in choosing the appropriate fiscal policy, policy makers balance short-term considerations related to macroeconomic stabilization with long-term considerations about the costs of debt. A common view among economists is that the government should run deficits when the economy is far below full employment and balanced budgets or surpluses when the economy is near full employment. The deficit has already declined markedly from historically high levels in fiscal years 2009 to 2011, but a structural deficit remains that is projected to grow over time under current policy.[44] Thus, many economists advocate further deficit reduction (fiscal austerity) as the economy nears full employment. This view has often been expressed as a prescription of deficit-reduction in the medium term (i.e., when the economy is near full employment), but not the short term.[45]

Likewise, the Fed has followed a policy of monetary stimulus since the financial crisis—reducing the federal funds rate to near zero and engaging in large-scale asset purchases—in an attempt to hasten a return to full employment.[46] The Fed has already scaled back its asset purchases and has stated: "In determining how long to maintain the current 0 to 1/4 percent target range for the federal funds rate, the Committee will assess progress—both realized and expected—toward its objectives of maximum employment and 2 percent inflation."[47] In other words, the Fed intends to raise interest rates only when it judges the economy to be closer to full employment.

The current unemployment rate would seemingly call for a near-term tightening of fiscal and monetary policy. For example, from December 2012 to January 2014, the Fed's announced policy was that it would keep interest rates "exceptionally low" at least until the unemployment rate reached 6.5%—which is close to current levels.[48]

The preponderance of evidence suggests that the economy is not as close to full employment as the current unemployment rate might suggest. For that reason, the Fed decided in March 2014 to drop its threshold unemployment rate of 6.5% from its forward guidance of when it would raise interest rates.[49] In a press conference following the decision, Fed Chair Janet Yellen provided this explanation of the Fed's decision:

> We initially started with an unemployment rate as a threshold. That was easy enough for the Committee to say, "With an unemployment rate above 61/2 percent, we know we're not close to full employment, not close to an employment level consistent with our mandate, and unless inflation were a significant concern, we wouldn't dream of raising the federal funds rate target." Now, the Committee has never felt that the unemployment rate is a sufficient statistic for the labor market. I think if I had to choose one indicator of the labor market, the unemployment rate is probably as good a one as I could find. But in assessing the real state of slack in the labor market and ultimately of inflationary pressures that might—or deflationary pressures that could result from that—it's appropriate to look at many more things. And that's why the Committee now states we will look at a broad range of information.[50]

Divergence between the unemployment rate and other indicators complicates formulating and communicating a policy response. If there is still considerable slack in the economy, despite the decline in the unemployment rate, then tightening policy could be premature and there is less concern that continued stimulus would cause inflation to rise. That evaluation could be proven wrong, however, if there turns out to be less slack in the economy than most economists currently estimate. This would be the case if structural changes or the Great Recession (i.e., hysteresis) permanently reduced the potential capacity of output and labor markets, so that the economy is no longer capable of returning to the historical trend.[51] In this scenario, microeconomic structural policy measures (e.g., spending or tax provisions that increase the incentives to hire, seek work, delay retirement, or train) are more likely to have positive results than fiscal or monetary stimulus.[52] For example, if the natural rate of unemployment is now higher, fiscal or monetary stimulus to reduce unemployment to levels attained in previous expansions and maintain price stability would, by definition, not be successful.[53] If the economy is getting close to full employment (because the economy's productive potential is lower than projected), then continued stimulus would in theory cause inflation to rise. If policy makers were to wait to tighten policy until inflation starts rising, it might be too late to achieve full employment and maintain price stability, due to lags in the effects of policy changes on the economy. As this example illustrates, some economists see the risks of choosing an unsuitable macroeconomic policy stance based on incomplete and contradictory data as an argument against pursuing activist macroeconomic policies.

End Notes

[1] For an overall analysis of the economic recovery, see CRS Report R41332, Economic Recovery: Sustaining U.S. Economic Growth in a Post-Crisis Economy, by Craig K. Elwell.

[2] This issue is analyzed in greater depth in CRS Report R41785, The Increase in Unemployment Since 2007: Is It Cyclical or Structural?, by Craig K. Elwell.

[3] Recessions are determined by the National Bureau of Economic Research. It defines a recession as "a significant decline in economic activity [that] spreads across the economy and can last from a few months to more than a year." See National Bureau of Economic Research, Statement of the NBER Business Cycle Dating Committee on the Determination of the Dates of Turning Points in the U.S. Economy, webpage, http://www.nber.org/cycles/general_statement.html.

[4] The first time was from 1982 to 1983, when unemployment peaked at 10.8%.

[5] CBO data available at http://cbo.gov/publication/45068.

[6] Therefore, economists sometimes refer to the natural rate as the non-accelerating inflation rate of unemployment (NAIRU) or the full employment rate of unemployment.

[7] Fed estimates are available at http://federalreserve.gov/monetarypolicy/files/ fomcprojtabl 20131218.pdf.

[8] CBO data available at http://cbo.gov/publication/45068.

[9] CRS calculations based on CBO data.

[10] Christopher Erceg and Andrew Levin, "Labor Force Participation and Monetary Policy in the Wake of the Great Recession," International Monetary Fund, working paper no. 13/245, December 2013, p. 20, available at http://www.bostonfed.org/employment2013/papers/ Erceg_Levin_Session1.pdf.

[11] Congressional Budget Office, The Slow Recovery of the Labor Market, February 2014, p. 1, available at http://www.cbo.gov/publication/45011.

[12] Precisely how close the current unemployment rate is to the natural rate depends on whether the natural rate has increased in recent years—an issue discussed in the section below entitled "A Rising Natural Rate of Unemployment?"

[13] CPS data accessed in February 2014, available at http://data.bls.gov/pdq/querytool.jsp? survey=ln. According to the CES, job growth averaged 194,000 per month in 2013, slightly higher than in 2011 and 2012. As noted above, unemployment data cannot be directly compared to employment data from the CES. CES data accessed in February 2014, available at http://data.bls.gov/pdq/querytool.jsp?survey=ce.

[14] This period is analyzed in Robert Moffitt, "The Reversal of the Employment-Population Ratio in the 2000s," Brookings Papers on Economic Activity, Fall 2012, available at http://www.brookings.edu/~/media/Projects/BPEA/ Fall%202012/2012b_Moffitt.pdf.

[15] One study characterizes the labor force participation rate as "weakly pro-cyclical." See Willem Van Zandweghe, "Interpreting the Recent Decline in Labor Force Participation," Federal Reserve Bank of Kansas City, Economic Review, First Quarter 2012, p. 9, available at http://www.kc.frb.org/publicat/econrev/pdf/12q1VanZandweghe.pdf.

[16] Willem Van Zandweghe, "Interpreting the Recent Decline in Labor Force Participation," Federal Reserve Bank of Kansas City, Economic Review, First Quarter 2012, p. 7, available at http://www.kc.frb.org/publicat/econrev/pdf/ 12q1VanZandweghe.pdf.

[17] For more information, see the section below entitled "Youth Employment and Unemployment."

[18] Hui Shan and Jari Stehn, "Young vs. Old as Drivers of Labor Force Participation," Goldman Sachs U.S. Daily Newsletter, February 11, 2014.

[19] Heidi Shierholz, "Most of the Decline in Labor Force Participation in the Last Six Years is Cyclical," The Economic Policy Institute Blog, February 21, 2014, available at http://www.epi.org/blog/decline-labor-force-participation-years/.

[20] Attempts to explain a phenomenon after it occurs are vulnerable to problems of confusing correlation with causality. As a check against this, it is interesting to note that, in its 2007 projection, BLS projected the labor force participation rate would fall by only 0.3 percentage points by 2012. According to one study, the BLS projections were accurate for older workers, but did not predict any decline in the participation rate of prime age workers or as large a decline in young workers. See Christopher Erceg and Andrew Levin, "Labor Force Participation and Monetary Policy in the Wake of the Great Recession," International Monetary Fund, working paper no. 13/245, December 2013, p. 11, available at http://www. bostonfed.org/employment2013/papers/Erceg_Levin_Session1.pdf.

[21] Although the participation rate of older workers has not fallen, since there are relatively more older workers and their participation rate is relatively lower than that of prime age workers,

the overall participation rate has fallen. One criticism of some of these studies is that because they are not adjusting for the fact that baby boomer women have a higher participation rate than earlier cohorts, they are overestimating the contribution of demographics to the recent decline in the labor force participation rate. See Heidi Shierholz, "Most of the Decline in Labor Force Participation in the Last Six Years is Cyclical," The Economic Policy Institute Blog, February 21, 2014, available at http://www.epi.org/blog/decline-labor-force-participation-years/.

[22] See Congressional Budget Office, The Slow Recovery of the Labor Market, February 2014, p. 11, available at http://www.cbo.gov/publication/45011; Christopher Erceg and Andrew Levin, "Labor Force Participation and Monetary Policy in the Wake of the Great Recession," International Monetary Fund, working paper no. 13/245, December 2013, pp. 17-18, available at http://www.bostonfed.org/employment2013/papers/Erceg_Levin_Session1.pdf; Morgan Stanley, "Explaining the Exodus in Labor Force Participation," U.S. Economics Newsletter, January 29, 2014.

[23] See Julie Hotchkiss, Melinda Pitts, and Fernando Rios-Avila, "A Closer Look at Nonparticipants During and After the Great Recession," Federal Reserve Bank of Atlanta, working paper no. 2012-10, August 2012, available at http://www.frbatlanta.org/documents/pubs/wp/wp1210.pdf; and Hui Shan and Jari Stehn, "Young vs. Old as Drivers of Labor Force Participation," Goldman Sachs U.S. Daily Newsletter, February 11, 2014.

[24] Goldman Sachs views the negative correlation between employment growth and labor force participation at the state level as evidence that the decline is cyclical. See David Mericle, "A State-Level Look at Declining Labor Force Participation," Goldman Sachs U.S. Daily Newsletter, April 17 2013.

[25] Individuals who are discouraged or marginally attached to the labor force are not included in the official definition of unemployment.

[26] One study argues that the increase in disability claimants is structural and not cyclical because the long-term upward trend in claimants showed no acceleration during or since the Great Recession. Dave Reifschneider, William Wascher, and David Wilcox, "Aggregate Supply in the United States," working paper presented at the International Monetary Fund research conference, November 7, 2013, p. 23, available at https://www.imf.org/external/np/res/seminars/2013/ arc/pdf/wilcox.pdf. Another study points to the increase in new claimants (i.e., the incremental increase, rather than the trend) during the recession as signs that disability claims were affected by the recession. The increase was reversed in the economic recovery. James Sherk, "Not Looking for Work," Heritage Foundation, Backgrounder, no. 2722, September 5, 2013, available at http://www.heritage.org/research/reports/2013/09/not-looking-for-work-why-laborforce-participation-has-fallen-during-the-recession.

[27] The increase in the numerator (number unemployed) and denominator (number in the labor force) left the unemployment rate unchanged.

[28] According to Social Security Administration data, among individuals who had their disability benefits terminated in 2012, about 90% had benefits terminated because they either died or reached federal retirement age. U.S. Social Security Administration, Annual Statistical Supplement, 2013 Table 6.F2, available at http://www.ssa.gov/policy/docs/ statcomps/supplement/2013/6f.html#table6.f2.

[29] Congressional Budget Office, The Slow Recovery of the Labor Market, Feb. 2014, p. 11, available at http://www.cbo.gov/publication/45011.

[30] Congressional Budget Office, The Slow Recovery of the Labor Market, February 2014, p. 2, available at http://www.cbo.gov/publication/45011.

[31] Alan Krueger, Judd Cramer, and David Cho, "Are the Long-Term Unemployed on the Margins of the Labor Market?", Brookings Papers on Economic Activity, March 2014, available at http://www.brookings.edu/~/media/projects/bpea/spring%202014/2014a_krueger; and Rand Ghayad, "The Jobless Trap," working paper, 2013, available at http://media.wix.com/ugd/576e9a_f6cf3b6661e44621ad26547112f66691.pdf.

[32] Labor force participation rates for ages 16 to 24 were the lowest ever recorded in 2012.

[33] Julie Hotchkiss, Melinda Pitts, and Fernando Rios-Avila, "A Closer Look at Nonparticipants During and After the Great Recession," Federal Reserve Bank of Atlanta, working paper no. 2012-10, Aug. 2012, p. 5, available at http://www.frbatlanta.org/documents/ pubs/wp/wp1210.pdf. See also Joyce Kwok et al., "Labor Force Participation and the Future Path of Unemployment," Federal Reserve Bank of San Francisco, Economic Letter, no. 2010-27, September 13, 2010. This study found that "the percentage of teenagers enrolled in school but not participation in the labor force has gone from about 40% to almost 60% over the past 25 years."

[34] Eric Rosengren, "Labor Market Slack and Monetary Policy, speech before the Boston Economic Club, February 26, 2014, available at http://www.bostonfed.org/news/speeches /rosengren/2014/022614/022614text.pdf.

[35] See, for example, Brad Delong, "Hysteresis and the American Unemployment Problem," blog post, January 31, 2012, available at http://delong.typepad.com/sdj/2012/01/hysteresis-and-the-american-unemployment-problem.html; Dave Reifschneider, William Wascher, and David Wilcox, "Aggregate Supply in the United States," working paper presented at the International Monetary Fund research conference, November 7, 2013, p. 22, available at https://www.imf.org/external/np/res/seminars/2013/arc/pdf/wilcox.pdf.

[36] Given the recent behavior of the unemployment and labor force participation rates, hysteresis could arguably be affecting the latter measure more than the former. As workers become discouraged and leave the labor force, they no longer exert upward pressure on the natural rate of unemployment because they are no longer officially unemployed.

The atypically high rate of long-term unemployment provides a potential avenue for increased hysteresis in the LFPR if the long-term unemployed continue to drop out of the labor force in the future.

[37] See Olivier Blanchard and Lawrence Summers, "Hysteresis in Unemployment," European Economic Review, vol. 31, no. 1/2, 1987, p. 288; and Laurence Ball, "Hysteresis in Unemployment: Old and New Evidence," National Bureau of Economic Research, working paper, no. 14818, March 2009.

[38] By comparison, the actual unemployment rate ranged from 4.4% to 4.7% at the end of the previous economic expansion.

[39] Congressional Budget Office, The Slow Recovery of the Labor Market, February 2014, p. 7, available at http://www.cbo.gov/publication/45011.

[40] CBO data available at http://cbo.gov/publication/45068.

[41] According to one study: "A longstanding and well-established fact in labor economics is that the labor supply of prime-age and older adults has been essentially acyclical throughout the postwar period, while that of teenagers has been moderately procyclical.... Consequently, macroeconomists have largely focused on the unemployment rate as a business cycle indicator while abstracting from movements in labor force participation.... " Christopher Erceg and Andrew Levin, "Labor Force Participation and Monetary Policy in the Wake of the Great Recession," International Monetary Fund, working paper no. 13/245, December 2013, p. 1, available at http://www.bostonfed.org/ employment2013/papers/Erceg_Levin_Session1.pdf.

[42] The output gap is the difference between actual GDP and potential GDP. It is an attempt to quantify the slack in the economy relative to GDP and is independently estimated by various forecasters.

[43] For a recap of the use of fiscal policy since the recession, see CRS Report R41578, Unemployment: Issues in the 113th Congress, by Jane G. Gravelle.

[44] Congressional Budget Office, The Budget and Economic Outlook, March 2014; Congressional Budget Office, The 2013 Long-Term Budget Outlook, September 2013. The budget deficit automatically grows when the economy falls below full employment and shrinks when the economy approaches full employment. The structural deficit is an estimate of the underlying deficit that remains when these cyclical factors are removed.

[45] See, for example, International Monetary Fund, United States: 2013 Article IV Consultation, IMF Country Report, no. 13/236, July 2013, http://www.imf.org/external/pubs/ft/scr/2013/cr13236.pdf; The National Commission on Fiscal Responsibility and Reform, The Moment of Truth, December 2010, p. 12, available at http://www.fiscalcommission.gov/sites/fiscalcommission.gov/files/documents/TheMomentofTruth12_1_2010.pdf. Macroeconomic stabilization reasons to delay deficit reduction to the medium term can be weighed against other reasons for short-term reduction, such as the pressures put on elderly entitlement programs by the aging of the population.

[46] For more information, see CRS Report R42962, Federal Reserve: Unconventional Monetary Policy Options, by Marc Labonte.

[47] Federal Reserve, "Federal Reserve Issues FOMC Statement," press release, March 19, 2014, http://federalreserve.gov/newsevents/press/monetary/20140319a.htm.

[48] From January to March 2014, the Fed modified this language to read that "it likely will be appropriate to maintain the current ... federal funds rate well past the time that the unemployment rate declines below 61/2%.... " Federal Reserve, "Federal Reserve Issues FOMC Statement," press release, January 29, 2014, available at http://federalreserve.gov/newsevents/press/monetary/20140129a.htm.

[49] Federal Reserve, "Federal Reserve Issues FOMC Statement," press release, March 19, 2014, available at http://federalreserve.gov/newsevents/press/monetary/20140319a.htm.

[50] The Federal Reserve press conference transcript is available at http://federalreserve.gov/mediacenter/files/ FOMCpresconf20140319.pdf.

[51] In other words, potential output and labor supply is higher today than it was before the Great Recession, but not as high as it would have been had the Great Recession not occurred. One study estimates that potential output has been reduced by 63/4% at the end of 2013 compared to what it would have been. Despite this decline in potential output, the study's authors estimate that significant slack remains in the economy. See Dave Reifschneider, William Wascher, and David Wilcox, "Aggregate Supply in the United States," working paper presented at the International Monetary Fund research conference, November 7, 2013, available at https://www.imf.org/external/np/res/seminars/2013/arc/pdf/ wilcox.pdf.

[52] A discussion of these microeconomic measures are beyond the scope of this report. For more information, see CRS Report 92-939, Countercyclical Job Creation Programs, by Linda Levine; and CRS Report R43044, Expediting the Return to Work: Approaches in the Unemployment Compensation Program, by Julie M. Whittaker; and CRS Report R42018, The Role of Public Works Infrastructure in Economic Recovery, by Claudia Copeland, Linda Levine, and William J. Mallett.

[53] If the economy's productive potential were still being eroded for as long as the economy remains below full employment, this would be another rationale for stimulative policies. In this context, some economists have argued that temporarily higher than desired inflation

could be worthwhile if it brought the economy back to full employment faster, thereby avoiding further hysteresis and erosion of potential output. It is less clear, however, whether more stimulus could successfully reverse the effects (if any) of hysteresis that have already occurred since the Great Recession.

In: The Labor Force Participation Rate
Editor: Darrel Graves
ISBN: 978-1-63463-391-8

Chapter 3

THE INCREASE IN UNEMPLOYMENT SINCE 2007: IS IT CYCLICAL OR STRUCTURAL?*

Linda Levine

SUMMARY

The unemployment rate greatly increased after the onset of the latest recession in December 2007, when it measured 5.0%. The rate peaked at 10.0% in October 2009, four months after the recession's official end in June 2009. More than three years into the recovery, the unemployment rate averaged 8.1% in 2012. Given its still elevated level, policymakers may continue to be concerned about how to spur economic growth and create jobs.

Over the past few years, Congress has used fiscal policy and the Federal Reserve (Fed) has used monetary policy to put the economy on a path toward the level of demand for goods and services that preceded the 2007-2009 recession. Firms react to recessions by laying off workers, and the deeper the downturn in the business cycle, the greater the rise in unemployment that results. Expansionary fiscal and monetary policies commonly have been used to remedy what is known as cyclical unemployment.

* This is an edited, reformatted and augmented version of Congressional Research Service Publication, No. R41785, dated January 24, 2013.

The unemployment rate has not been as responsive as had been hoped to the countercyclical measures undertaken by Congress and the Fed. Consequently, some have suggested that an increase in another type of unemployment—referred to as structural unemployment—has accounted for much of the rise in the unemployment rate from pre-recession levels. These observers assert that the rise in unemployment due to change in the structure of the economy represents "a new normal" of elevated unemployment rates for years to come.

Structural unemployment develops for different reasons than cyclical unemployment. Structural unemployment results when jobseekers do not move quickly into vacant jobs. Obstacles that lengthen the spell of unemployment (i.e., prolong the period of job search) include mismatches between the skills or locations of jobless workers and the skill requirements or locations of available jobs. Another impediment is the composition of the unemployed, such as more workers whose connection to their former employers is permanently severed (i.e., fewer workers likely to be recalled from layoffs once business revives at their former employers). A third factor that may contribute to long-term unemployment is known as labor market institutions, such as unemployment benefit programs.

The measures enacted by Congress have chiefly focused on alleviating cyclical unemployment. To the extent that the still-high unemployment rate results from the slow pace of output growth during the recovery, economic theory suggests that fiscal and monetary stimulus would be suitable strategies for further reducing joblessness. To the extent that structural factors have contributed to the still-high unemployment rate, economic theory suggests measures such as promoting the education and retraining of workers who permanently lost jobs in hard-hit industries (e.g., home building) so that they can acquire the skills needed to obtain employment in other industries.

This report assesses the relative magnitudes of cyclical and structural unemployment as they respond to different policy measures. An analysis of changes since 2007 in a variety of labor market indicators across industries and areas finds patterns that strongly suggest most of the increase in the U.S. unemployment rate is cyclical (i.e., due to depressed aggregate demand). Empirical studies suggest that, although structural unemployment has temporarily increased, it accounted for a minority of the rise in the unemployment rate in recent years.

INTRODUCTION

During the past few years, economists have been debating how much of the increase in unemployment since the start of the 2007-2009 recession is due to reduced demand for goods and services compared with compositional changes entailing worker reallocation across industries and areas.[1] In other words, how much of the increase in the official unemployment rate from 5.0% at the recession's outset in December 2007 to a peak of 10.0% in October 2009 was cyclical unemployment and how much was structural unemployment?

Distinguishing cyclical from structural unemployment is more than an academic exercise. Their relative contribution to the increase in the unemployment rate since 2007 has different implications for the pace at which the economy can grow without spurring inflation and for which public policies are most appropriate to lower an unemployment rate that remains elevated long after the latest recession's end in June 2009.

Many workers who became unemployed during the 2007-2009 recession are expected to return to jobs in their former industries as demand for the goods and services they previously produced grows during the recovery phase of the business cycle. Fiscal and monetary policies often have been used to jump-start aggregate demand and job growth for the cyclically unemployed. In response to the latest recession, for example, recent Congresses enacted multiple measures to stimulate demand and promote job creation while the Federal Reserve (Fed) undertook various strategies to mitigate the financial crisis that coincided with the recession and to stimulate economic activity.[2] If the increase in unemployment is largely due to the sluggish pace of output growth since the recession's end, then economic theory suggests that fiscal and monetary stimulus would be suitable strategies for lowering the unemployment rate from its still-elevated average of 8.1% in 2012.

Those workers who permanently lost their jobs during the 2007-2009 recession are expected to experience a longer spell of unemployment than those temporarily laid off until product demand revives in their former sectors of employment. The duration of job losers' unemployment may be further lengthened if the skills they possess do not match the skills required by jobs in growing sectors or if they live in areas different from those experiencing job growth. To overcome skill mismatch for example, displaced workers may require retraining or additional formal education. Congress recognized that different public policies are appropriate for helping structurally unemployed workers return to economically productive activities when it included training provisions among the countercyclical measures in the American Recovery and Reinvestment Act, for example.[3]

Rather than persisting in their search for jobs, some structurally unemployed workers may drop out of the labor force, thereby reducing the supply of labor and the capacity of the economy to grow in the long run.[4] A smaller labor force also reduces income tax payments and imposes additional costs on society. For example, because older workers, the partially disabled and less educated are among those most likely to stop participating in the labor force, early claiming of Society Security retirement benefits and entering the Social Security Disability Income program could increase.[5]

Given the different implications of cyclical and structural unemployment for policymakers, this report distinguishes between the relative magnitude of the two in recent years. Before conducting this analysis, the report defines a few concepts that will help the reader navigate the remainder of the report.

A Few Concepts Briefly Explained

Economists often break down unemployment into three types: frictional, structural, and cyclical.

- *Frictional* unemployment arises from the ever-present movement of people into and out of jobs. Examples include the unemployment of college graduates while searching for their first jobs, of family caregivers returning to the labor force, and of workers who quit jobs before having found new ones. Both frictional and structural unemployment involve the worker-to-job matching process. Two distinctions between them are the voluntary nature of some frictional unemployment and its shorter duration compared with structural unemployment.
- *Structural* unemployment arises from obstacles to the worker-to-job-matching process that lengthen unemployment spells. Impediments to unemployed workers quickly moving to firms with available jobs include mismatches (between the skills or locations of jobless workers and the skill requirements or locations of available jobs), the composition of the unemployed (toward workers who permanently lost jobs vis-a-vis workers temporarily laid off, for example), and the characteristics of labor market institutions (such as the wage-replacement rate and duration of unemployment benefits).
- *Cyclical* unemployment arises when the economy experiences a decrease in the demand for goods and services. Employers adjust to a downturn in the business cycle by temporarily laying off workers and cutting the hours of employees retained to fill reduced product

demand. When demand starts to revive, firms may be reluctant to immediately resume hiring and may first increase the hours of their existing work force. Once firms feel confident that economic growth will continue, they recall the experienced workers laid off during the recession.

Under certain conditions, however, cyclical unemployment may evolve into structural unemployment. If the economy grows slowly for an extended period after a recession's end and causes the unemployment rate to remain high for quite some time, then some of what began as cyclical unemployment may become structural unemployment. The following is an example of how this occurs. By definition, the skills of the cyclically unemployed at the outset of their displacement match the skills demanded by employers. But the longer these workers remain jobless, the greater the likelihood their skills will become rusty. As economic growth strengthens and firms start hiring workers, the skills of the long-term unemployed may have so deteriorated that they no longer match the skill requirements of available jobs.

Frictional, structural, and cyclical unemployment are not directly measured, but policy analysts have estimated the nonaccelerating inflation rate of unemployment (NAIRU). Because the NAIRU is estimated without regard to fluctuations in aggregate demand (i.e., without regard to the business cycle), it commonly is used as a proxy for the structural unemployment rate. The NAIRU or natural rate of unemployment reflects the extent of long-term slack in the labor market, which is helpful to know when formulating policy. For example, a substantial increase in structural unemployment implies that there is much less excess labor (capacity) in the economy. Consequently, the Fed cannot reduce the official unemployment rate as much as it previously could without raising the inflation rate.

CYCLICAL VS. STRUCTURAL UNEMPLOYMENT

Based on the following analysis of changes in multiple labor market indicators by industry and area, a majority of the increase in unemployment between the 2007-2009 recession's onset and its peak in 2010 appears to be cyclical. As discussed in detail below, this finding is supported by several empirical studies which estimated that any increase in structural unemployment that occurred accounted for a minority of the rise in the U.S.

unemployment rate. The results do not suggest that the nation is facing a "new normal" of elevated unemployment rates for years to come.

Evidence of Greatly Increased Cyclical Unemployment

> The mismatch argument for sustained increases in the unemployment rate and the NAIRU is predicated on imbalances in labor supply and demand across sectors and skill groups. The extent of such imbalances can be assessed by examining employment growth and unemployment rates across industry sectors, states, and occupations.[6]

This approach is pursued below using annual average data from 2007 to 2010, the year in which the unemployment rate peaked at 9.6%.

Job Loss by Industry and Unemployment Rates by State

The 7.8 million jobs lost between 2007 and 2010 occurred across a broad swath of industries.[7] The number of jobs on employers' payrolls plummeted in 18 of the 24 industries shown in **Figure 1**. Cyclically sensitive industries, such as manufacturing and construction, bore the brunt of job losses during the latest recession just as they did during prior recessions. When aggregate employment stopped declining in March 2010, "the dispersion of employment gains and losses across sectors returned to its pre-recession level, suggesting very little imbalance in the pace of employment growth at that point."[8]

The data displayed in **Figure 1** support DeLong's statement that "What we have witnessed is not a shift in demand into sectors lacking an adequate number of qualified and productive workers, but rather a collapse in the level of aggregate demand."[9] He concluded that, as of fall 2010, evidence was lacking of "labor shortages, rising wages, and increasing prices in expanding sectors, accompanied by high unemployment elsewhere in the economy," which would be the case if skills mismatch was the major explanation for the nation's high unemployment rate. DeLong went on to note, however, that were unemployment to remain high "for two or three more years" then structural unemployment could well become a bigger factor because "nothing converts cyclical unemployment into structural unemployment more certainly than prolonged unemployment."

Just as job losses occurred in most industries between 2007 and 2010, so too did the unemployment rate rise in every state in the nation.[10] The across-the-board increase in unemployment rates suggests that labor demand fell throughout the country, belying the notion of a mismatch between the locations of available jobs and workers desiring employment.

Only two states—Alaska (6,500 jobs) and North Dakota (17,200 jobs)—and the District of Columbia (17,100 jobs) posted net employment gains between 2007 and 2010.[11] This implies that unemployed workers had little incentive to move to find jobs, which does not support speculation that conditions in the housing market dampened the migration rate of unemployed homeowners.

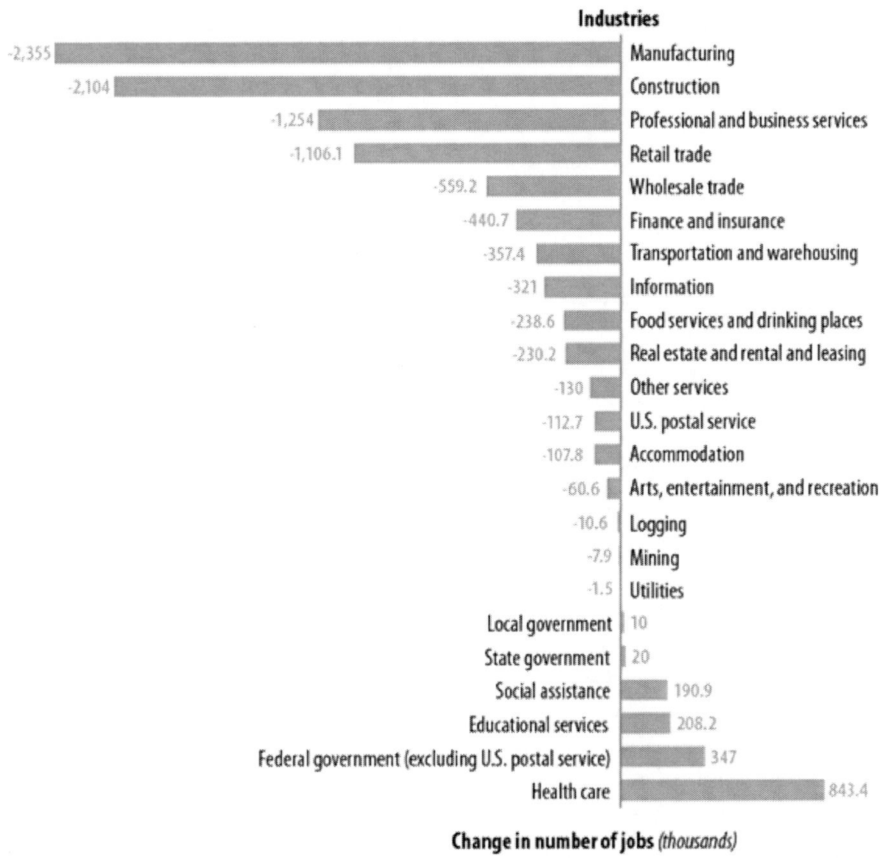

Source: Created by CRS from the total number of nonfarm jobs in 2007 and 2010, according to U.S. Bureau of Labor Statistics data from the Current Employment Statistics program.

Figure 1. Change in the Number of Jobs by Industry, 2007-2010.

Most empirical analyses also suggest that the state of the housing market is not an especially good explanation for the decrease in geographic mobility since 2007.[12] Molloy, Smith, and Wozniak found neither the housing market contraction nor the 2007-2009 recession to be persuasive reasons for the recent decrease in internal migration rates.[13] Kaplan and Schulhofer-Wohl determined that the large drop in annual interstate migration rates starting in 2006, which had led some observers to infer a connection to "house lock," was instead the result of a change in the Census Bureau's procedure for imputing missing data in the Current Population Survey (CPS). Kaplan and Schulhofer-Wohl considered the smaller change in migration rates from two other sources (the Census Bureau's American Community Survey and the Internal Revenue Service) to bolster their assessment that interstate migration has not recently decreased to a substantial degree.[14]

Using data from yet another source (the Census Bureau's Survey of Income and Program Participation), Aaronson and Davis estimated that the decrease in state-to-state migration rates during the 2007-2009 recession and the first year of recovery were similar for homeowners and renters and also were similar to their experience during prior recessions. They further found little empirical support for the house lock argument based on the severity of a state's decline in housing prices or the unemployment status of the head of homeowner households.[15]

Schmitt and Warner took a different approach to determining whether differences in housing market conditions by state affected the geographic mobility of job losers. They estimated that the probability of displaced workers' moving over the 2007-2009 period was little affected by differences in housing market performance across states.[16] Displaced workers in Nevada, California, Florida, Arizona, and Michigan—which were among the 10 states to experience the largest decreases in a statewide housing price index—had almost the same likelihood of not moving after losing their jobs (90.7%) as displaced workers in the 10 states with the best housing markets (91.5%).[17]

Using monthly microdata from the Current Population Survey and an econometric model, Valletta found no evidence in favor of the house-lock argument. Because house lock would mean a longer period of job search in the local labor market for owners of homes whose values had decreased, he examined differences in unemployment durations between homeowners and renters across metropolitan areas differentiated by their degree of decreases in home prices. The results of his analysis do not support the hypothesis that reduced geographic mobility among homeowners contributed to high unemployment during the recession and through 2011.[18]

Alternatively, based on their construction of a model of metropolitan area housing and labor markets and migration, Karahan and Rhee concluded that house lock reduced geographic mobility and exacerbated the increase in unemployment during the Great (2007-2009) Recession.[19] They estimated that, absent the housing bust, workers would have been more likely to move during the recession from areas with higher to lower unemployment rates (the migration rate would have risen). As a result, the decline in migration shown in the various data sources referenced above understated the impact of the sharp drop in house prices on worker mobility and unemployment. Geographic mismatch resulting from the housing bust may explain about 0.5 percentage points of the increase in the unemployment rate during the 2007-2009 recession, according to Karahan and Rhee.

Underemployment by Industry

Firms can adjust the quantity of labor they use in response to a decrease in aggregate demand not only by reducing the size of their work forces but also by cutting the hours of qualified employees they retain on their payrolls. The latter action produces "underemployment," that is, workers employed part-time who would prefer to be employed full-time but cannot for economic reasons (e.g., unfavorable business conditions).[20] Because underemployment reflects the demand for workers who possess the skills required to perform their jobs, analysis of changes in underemployment takes skill mismatch out of the equation.

The demand for qualified employees fell across every industry shown in **Figure 2**. The total number of underemployed workers slightly more than doubled over the three-year period to 8.9 million in 2010, when the unemployment rate reached its most recent peak.[21] Underemployment increased even more so in the following diverse group of industries: retail trade; social assistance; food services and drinking places; health care; accommodation; arts, entertainment, and recreation; educational services; and state government.

Jayadev and Konczal analyzed the trend in underemployment from 2000 to 2010 for the construction and financial activities industries, and for all other industries. They found that the number of persons involuntarily working fewer than 35 hours a week had about doubled for both the construction and financial activities industries and for all other industries since the outset of the 2007-2009 recession, which coincided with a financial crisis related to the collapse of the housing market. Jayadev and Konczal took this as "a sign that underemployment is hitting every sector, not just those with hangovers from the bubble."[22] In other words, they believe this indicates that cyclical forces have primarily affected the labor market.

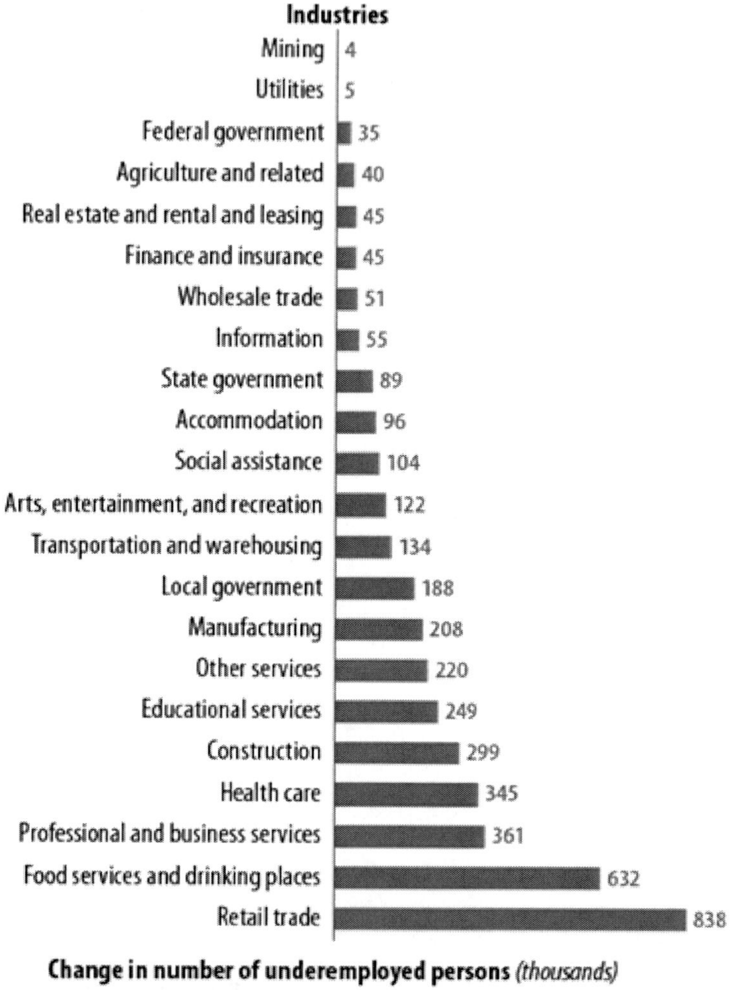

Source: Created by CRS from the total number of workers employed part-time for economic reasons in 2007 and 2010 according to U.S. Bureau of Labor Statistics data from the Current Population Survey.

Notes: Underemployed workers want to work full time but are working part-time (1-34 hours a week) for an economic reason (e.g., their hours were cut back or they were unable to find full-time jobs).

Figure 2. Change in the Number of Underemployed Workers by Industry, 2007-2010.

The Hiring Rate by Industry and Region

The decrease in the hiring rate (i.e., the number of hires as a percent of total nonfarm employment) between 2007 and 2010 in almost all industries for which data are available from the Job Openings and Labor Turnover Survey (JOLTS) again suggests the primacy of cyclical over structural factors.[23] (See **Figure 3**.) Employers in less than half of these industries hired relatively more workers in 2010 than in 2009. Rates returned to pre-recession levels in only construction[24] and the federal government.[25]

Offshore outsourcing, by changing the skill mix of jobs into which U.S. workers can be hired, has been offered as a reason for the slow recovery of the labor market. The largest declines in the hiring rate between 2007 and 2010 were in industries in which the major occupations are not especially vulnerable to offshoring, however. (Offshorable occupations have been defined as those whose duties do not require in-person contact between employees and customers or those whose duties do not have to be performed in the United States.)[26] Cooks, food preparation and serving workers (including fast food), and waiters and waitresses are among the leading occupations in the accommodations and food services industry, in which the hiring rate plunged 27.6 percentage points as shown in **Figure 3**.[27] Amusement and recreation attendants, fitness trainers and aerobics instructors, and landscaping and groundskeeping workers account for the largest shares of workers in the arts, entertainment and recreation industry, which experienced the second biggest decrease in the rate of hires. Counter and rental clerks; general maintenance and repair workers; property, real estate, and community association managers; and real estate sales agents are among the leading occupations in the real estate and rental and leasing industry, just as cashiers, retail salespersons, stock clerks, and order fillers are in the retail trade industry. Although some jobs in the finance and insurance industry may be more vulnerable to offshoring than the aforementioned jobs in industries whose hiring rate fell most precipitously between 2007 and 2010, tellers—a non-offshorable occupation—comprise the largest share of the finance and insurance industry's employment.

Just as hiring activity fell in most industries between 2007 and 2010, so too did hires drop in all four geographic areas for which JOLTS data are available. The West and South recorded the largest declines in the hiring rate (i.e., each fell by 11.7 percentage points to 36.1% and 37.3%, respectively).[28] Both regions include states that are among the most hard hit by the end of the housing bubble (e.g., Nevada and Florida). In the Midwest, the hiring rate decreased by 8.5 percentage points to 36.9% in 2010.[29] The Northeast's rate fell the least over the three-year period, decreasing by 4.7 percentage points to 34.3% in 2010.[30]

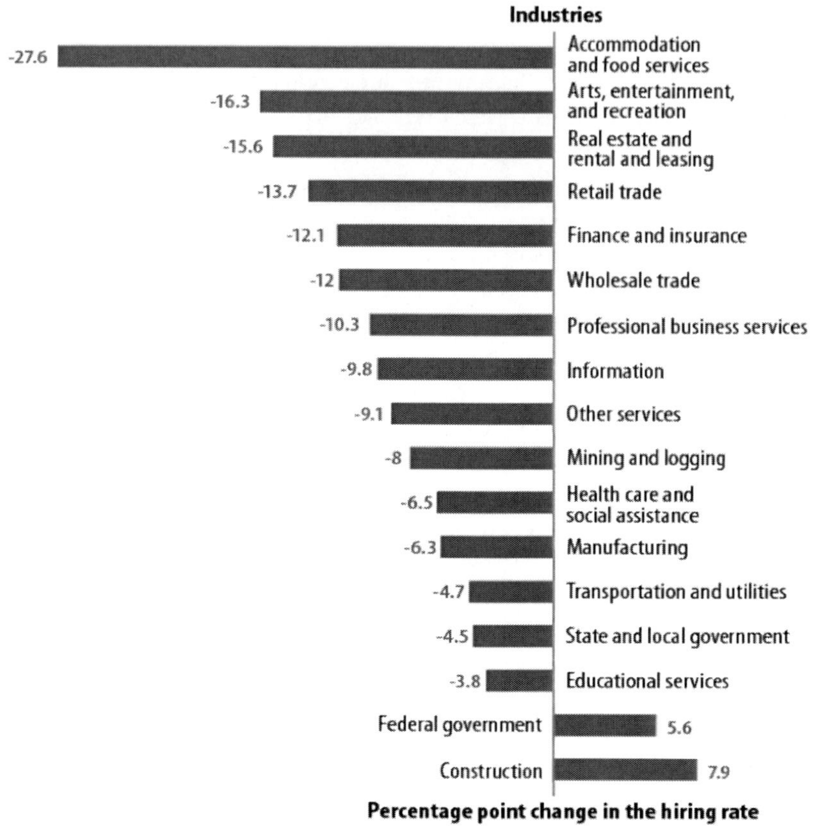

Source: Created by CRS from the hiring rate in 2007 and 2010 according to U.S. Bureau of Labor Statistics data from the Job Openings and Labor Turnover Survey.

Notes: The hiring rate is the number of hires during the entire year as a percent of annual average nonfarm employment.

Figure 3. Percentage Point Change in the Hiring Rate by Industry, 2007-2010.

The Ratio of Unemployed Workers to Job Openings by Industry

The number of unemployed workers for every job opening (vacancy) increased during the 2007- 2009 recession. From 1.8 unemployed workers per job opening at the recession's outset in December 2007, the ratio peaked at 6.7 in July 2009, one month after the recession ended.[31]

In late 2010, there were still about five unemployed workers for every job vacancy. The ratio has fallen slowly since then.[32]

With so many more jobseekers than available jobs it seems fairly straightforward for employers to transform vacancies into hires. But, the mismatch argument posits that employers are having difficulty filling vacancies because the skills unemployed workers possess do not qualify them for the available positions. The number of experienced (i.e., qualified) unemployed workers per job opening increased in every industry through 2010, however, when the unemployment rate mostly recently peaked at 9.6%.[33] (See **Table 1**.)

Sahin, Song, Topa, and Violante estimated that the rise in industry-level mismatch does not account for much of the increase in the unemployment rate and that the rise in mismatch was short-lived. Their analysis indicates that the increase in mismatch across industries explained between 0.59 and 0.75 percentage points of the rise in U.S. unemployment from its average of 4.6% in 2006, to its peak of 10.0% in October 2009, "i.e., at most 14 percent of the increase."[34] In 2010, the mismatch between unemployed workers and job vacancies across industries started moving toward pre-recession levels.

To some observers, the much higher ratio of unemployed workers to job openings in the construction industry compared with other industries in 2010 and the much higher ratio in the construction industry during the current recovery compared with the recovery from the 2001 recession suggest an increase in structural unemployment.[35] The latest recession was partly caused by the bursting of the housing bubble, before which high demand for homes drove up construction employment and likely held down the industry's ratio during the recovery from the 2001 recession.[36]

In addition, the existence of more qualified jobseekers than job openings in every industry shown in **Table 1** suggests that an economy-wide reduction in demand rather than shifts in demand across industries is the greater contributor to the increase in unemployment.

Lastly, even if many of the workers let go by residential building construction firms and residential specialty trade contractors face prolonged unemployment due to mismatch, the overall impact is likely to be limited because the two components of the construction industry accounted for only 2.4% of total nonfarm employment in 2005 (before the housing bubble burst).

Table 1. The Ratio of Experienced Unemployed Workers to Job Openings by Industry

Industry	Number of Experienced Unemployed Workers[a] Divided by Number of Job Openings[b]	
	December 2007	December 2010
Total private nonfarm industries	1.6	5.3
Mining and logging	1.3	3.7
Construction	9.7	51.4
Manufacturing	2.8	9.0
Wholesale and retail trade	1.8	7.7
Transportation and utilities	2.1	5.1
Information	1.5	3.4
Financial activities	1.2	3.0
Professional and business services	1.1	2.7
Education and health services	0.7	2.3
Leisure and hospitality	2.1	7.3
Other services	1.7	4.5
Government	1.1	2.6

Source: Calculated by CRS from Current Population Survey (CPS) and Job Openings and Labor Turnover Survey (JOLTS) data.

Notes: Comparable data on unemployment by industry from the CPS and on job openings by industry from JOLTS are available monthly on a not seasonally adjusted basis. When using not seasonally adjusted monthly data the appropriate comparison across time is month over year (e.g., December of 2007 and 2010).

[a] Experienced unemployed workers in a given industry are those workers who were employed in that industry just prior to separation from their employers. Persons who became unemployed upon entering or reentering the labor force are excluded.

[b] Job openings include only those positions for which employers are recruiting from outside their firms and for which work could start within 30 days regardless of when a suitable candidate is found.

Evidence of Somewhat Increased Structural Unemployment

Anomalies that occurred during the latest recession and ongoing recovery suggest that structural impediments to efficiently matching workers with jobs may have contributed more to the increase in the unemployment rate from 5.0% in December 2007 to a peak of 10.0% in October 2009 than they did during earlier fluctuations in the business cycle. These anomalies are the incidence of permanent job loss and of long-term unemployment as well as the nature of the relationship between unemployment and job vacancies. Most of the studies reviewed below estimated that any increase in structural unemployment in recent years accounted for a minority of the unemployment rate's rise, however. A few analyses further suggest that the recent increase in structural unemployment in the United States is unlikely to persist as occurred in some European countries starting in the 1980s and extending into the 1990s. Their conclusion that the U.S. labor market has not attained "a new normal" of high unemployment rates for years to come is partly due to the temporary nature of the Emergency Unemployment Compensation program enacted in 2008 and most recently extended by Congress through 2013.[37]

Permanent Job Loss and Long-Term Unemployment

"Two particularly worrisome signs suggestive of structural labor market problems ... are the concentration of the rise in unemployment among permanent job losers and the huge increase in long-term unemployment."[38] The unemployment rate may be higher than it otherwise would have been had the composition of unemployed workers not shifted toward the two hard-to-employ groups.

Workers who permanently lost their jobs (i.e., job losers *not* on temporary layoffs) grew from 1.7% of the labor force in 2007 to 5.1% in 2010, the year in which the unemployment rate most recently peaked.[39] In contrast, permanent job losers rose from 1.7% of the labor force in 1979 to just 4.0% in 1983 after the severe 1981-1982 recession.[40] Job losers' share of the labor force grew from 1.2% in 2000, before the start of the mild 2001 recession, to a much lower 2.6% in 2003 during the ensuing jobless recovery.

Temporary layoffs can be quickly reversed as the economy picks up steam, but job losses sever the employee-employer relationship and force job losers to search for new positions. Former employees of industries that may not soon see demand return to pre-recession levels (e.g., the residential construction industry) may experience especially lengthy unemployment if their skill sets do not match those of jobs in expanding sectors.[41]

More than six million workers were unemployed for longer than 27 weeks (i.e., the long-term unemployed) in 2010. They comprised over 40% of all workers unemployed in that and the two subsequent years. Earlier postwar peaks in the long-term unemployed's share of all unemployed workers were about half as large.[42] The long-term unemployment rate (i.e., persons unemployed more than six months as a share of the labor force) was 4.2% in 2010. At no other time during the postwar period was long-term unemployment more prevalent.[43]

Shimer estimated that the probability of reemployment decreases the longer workers remain unemployed in either good or bad economic times, but he also found that recessions result in the largest percentage decrease in the job-finding probability of the long-term unemployed.[44] Although it is unclear why the long-term unemployed have more difficulty getting jobs, some speculate that firms are reluctant to hire those toward the end of the unemployment queue because their skills may have atrophied from lack of use.[45] The long-term unemployed's chances of reemployment may also be depressed if their unemployment stigmatizes them in employers' eyes. In addition, workers may become demoralized after being jobless for a very long time and as a result, search less intensively for jobs.

Lazear and Spletzer concluded that the 11th postwar recession was not unlike earlier recessions— except more severe—with cyclical (transitory) factors largely accounting for the still-elevated unemployment rate. They noted that the high prevalence of long-term unemployment is an atypical feature of the Great Recession which "is not due to any observed structural change, but rather to the depth of the current recession."[46]

The Vacancy Rate and the Unemployment Rate

Yet a third anomaly suggestive of structural problems in the labor market is the nature of the relationship between the job vacancy (openings) rate and the unemployment rate after the recession's end in June 2009. Historically, there has been a stable negative association over the course of the business cycle between the vacancy rate (i.e., vacancies as a percentage of all filled and unfilled jobs) and the unemployment rate.[47] During economic expansions when demand is strong (i.e., the vacancy rate is high), the unemployment rate is low. During economic contractions when demand is weak (i.e., the vacancy rate is low), the unemployment rate is high.

The inverse relationship between the job openings and unemployment rates was maintained during the 2007-2009 recession, but both rates have increased during much of the recovery period. The unemployment rate averaged 2.6 percentage points higher in the January-March 2012 period than the rate predicted by their historically inverse relationship, according to Barnichon, Elsby, Hobijn and Sahin.[48] They also estimated that the higher than predicted unemployment rate was mostly due to the unusually low rate at which workers were hired to fill vacancies given the stage of the business cycle. Although the economists estimated that the shortfall in hires was present in many industries, the construction industry was found to have contributed most to the overall shortfall. Daly, Hobijn, Sahin, and Valletta suggested that if half of the unusually large number of construction workers who remain unemployed were to find jobs in other industries as the recovery proceeds, "the decline of construction would cause structural unemployment to increase by only about 0.4 percentage point."[49]

Estimates of the Increase in Structural Unemployment

Several economists estimated how much structural unemployment increased and contributed to the steep rise of the unemployment rate from a pre-recession average of 4.6% in 2007 to 9.3% in 2009 and a still higher 9.6% in 2010. Most of the empirical studies whose results are summarized in **Table 2** relied to varying degrees on recent deviations from the above-described negative relationship between vacancy and unemployment rates and from the positive relationship between the job-finding rate and the vacancy-unemployment ratio. Another difference that may affect their results is the time period covered by the analyses (e.g., ending in 2009 or 2010).

Six of the seven studies estimated an increase in structural unemployment that accounted for a minority of the recent rise in the unemployment rate. The results of these analyses imply that the increase in structural unemployment may explain between 20% and 35% (or 1.0-1.75 percentage points) of the 5 percentage point increase in the unemployment rate between 2007 and 2010.

Researchers disagree on the precise allocation of the unemployment rate's rise to skill as opposed to geographic mismatch. This likely relates in part to the different measures of mismatch they developed. Batini, Celasun, Dowling et al. estimated that their measure of skill mismatch by state raised structural unemployment by 1.0-1.75 percentage points between 2007 and 2009. (See **Table 2**.) In contrast, Estevao and Tsounta found that unfavorable conditions in the housing market (which may have reduced geographic mobility) accounted for more of their estimated 1.75 percentage point increase in structural unemployment over the 2006-2010 period than did skill mismatch (1 percentage point and 0.5 percentage point, respectively). Estevao and Tsounta estimated that the remaining rise in structural unemployment (0.25 percentage points) was due to the interaction of skill match with foreclosures. For their part, Sahin et al. found that geographic mismatch did not play a role in the unemployment rate's increase from 4.6% on average in 2006 to its October 2009 peak (10.0%), whereas mismatch across occupations explained between 0.6 and 0.9 percentage point of the rise.[50]

Table 2. Estimates of the Increase Since 2007 in the Structural Unemployment Rate

Percentage Point Increase in the Structural Unemployment Rate[a]	Author	Source
0.6-1.9, preferred estimate of 1.25	Mary Daly, Bart Hobijn, and Rob Valletta	The Recent Evolution of the Natural Rate of Unemployment, Federal Reserve Bank of San Francisco (FRBSF) Working Paper 2011-05, January 2011
1.0-1.75	Nicoletta Batini, Oya Celasun, Thomas Dowling, et al.	United States: Selected Issues Paper, International Monetary Fund, Country Report No. 10/248, July 2010
1.75	Marcello Estevao and Evridiki Tsounta	Has the Great Recession Raised U.S. Structural Unemployment?, IMF Working Paper 11/105, May 2011
1.7	Justin Weidner and John C. Williams	What Is the New Normal Unemployment Rate?, FRBSF Economic Letter 2011-05, February 14, 2011
1.5	Regis Barnichon and Andrew Figura	What Drives Movements in the Unemployment Rate?, Federal Reserve Board, Finance and Economics Discussion Series Working Paper 2010-48, August 20, 2010
2.5	Narayana Kocherlakota	Back Inside the FOMC, speech by the President of the Federal Reserve Bank of Minneapolis, September 8, 2010

Source: Created by CRS from the studies referenced in the table.

[a] There is no officially calculated rate of structural unemployment. The nonaccelerating inflation rate of unemployment (NAIRU) is a proxy for the structural unemployment rate because the NAIRU (or natural rate) is estimated without regard to fluctuations in aggregate demand.

The analysis of Herz and van Rens gave comparatively more weight to geographic than skills mismatch: they estimated that mismatch across states accounted for 0.1 percentage point of the 5 percentage point increase in unemployment during the Great Recession compared to 0.03 percentage point for skill mismatch.[51] Although Daly, Hobijn, and Valletta found that mismatch accounted for a larger share (0.5 percentage points or less) of their preferred estimated increase of 1.25 percentage points in structural unemployment from 2007 to 2010, it nonetheless explained a minority of the increase.

Empirical estimates of the impact of unemployment benefit extensions on the rise in structural unemployment are about equal to those for mismatch.[52] Differences between the researchers' estimates with regard to unemployment benefits likely reflects variations in how they operationalized the explanatory variable. Daly, Hobijn, and Valletta estimated that the temporarily authorized federal Emergency Unemployment Compensation (EUC) program accounted for 0.8 percentage points of the increase in structural unemployment from 2007 to 2010. Valletta and Kuang initially estimated a 0.4 percentage point increase in structural unemployment due to unemployment benefit extensions,[53] but after updating the data to include all of 2009 and the first half of 2010, the researchers found the effect of the EUC program to be twice as large (0.8 percentage points). Still others put the contribution of unemployment benefit extensions to increased unemployment at 0.3 percentage points,[54] 0.7-0.8 percentage points,[55] and at somewhat over 1 percentage point.[56]

Several analysts have speculated about whether the recent increase in structural unemployment will persist, thereby keeping the U.S. unemployment rate high for many years to come as occurred in some European countries from the 1980s into the 1990s.[57] Elsby, Hobijn, and Sahin stated that, despite the sharp decline in the U.S. job-finding rate, it remains well above the job-finding rates of many European countries that experienced a prolonged period of elevated structural unemployment starting in the 1980s.[58] While noting that their analysis does not suggest how long the 1.0-1.75 percentage point increase in structural unemployment due to mismatch will last, Batini, Celasun, Dowling et al. mentioned a distinctive feature of the U.S. economy—flexibility[59]—which may allow the United States to avoid stubbornly high unemployment rates for years to come.[60] Daly, Hobijn, and Valletta concluded that little of their 1.25 percentage point increase in structural unemployment is likely to persist "as labor market conditions improve [in the United States] and the extended UI provisions are allowed to expire."[61]

Taking into account changes over time in unemployment benefit programs and product market regulations, Guichard and Rusticelli estimated substantial differences in the vulnerability to structural unemployment increases among Organisation for Economic Cooperation and Development (OECD) nations.[62] Regardless of the unemployment effect of the financial crisis in the 28 OECD economies included in their 2010 study, Guichard and Rusticelli estimated that the United States may be less vulnerable than 20 nations to an increase in structural unemployment over the 2007-2012 period. Of the 10 OECD countries that experienced the largest unemployment impact from the recent financial crisis, they estimated that the United States was among the nations least vulnerable to an increase in structural unemployment.

End Notes

[1] See, for example, James Ledbetter, "Strucs vs. Cycs: The Two Gangs of Economists Warring Over the Causes of High Unemployment," *Slate*, August 24, 2010; and Prajakta Bhide, "The Fed Debates: Is Unemployment Structural or Cyclical?," *Forbes*, October 21, 2010.

[2] For additional information, see CRS Report R41578, *Unemployment: Issues in the 113th Congress*, by Jane G. Gravelle, Thomas L. Hungerford, and Linda Levine.

[3] For additional information, see CRS Report R40182, *Funding for Workforce Development in the American Recovery and Reinvestment Act (ARRA) of 2009*, by David H. Bradley and Ann Lordeman.

[4] Trend or potential economic (output) growth is dependent on the supply of labor and on productivity growth. For additional information, see CRS Report R42063, *Economic Growth and the Unemployment Rate*, by Linda Levine.

[5] Testimony of Till von Wachter, associate professor of Economics, Columbia University, in U.S. Congress, Senate Budget Committee, *Challenges for the U.S. Economic Recovery*, 112th Cong., 1st sess., February 3, 2011.

[6] Rob Valletta and Katherine Kuang, "Is Structural Unemployment on the Rise?," *FRBSF Economic Letter*, No. 2010- 34, November 8, 2010, p. 3. (Hereinafter cited as Valletta and Kuang, *Is Structural Unemployment on the Rise?*.)

[7] Calculated by CRS from the U.S. Bureau of Labor Statistics' (BLS) Current Employment Statistics (CES) program. National data from the CES program are available at http://stats.bls.gov/ces/.

[8] Valletta and Kuang, *Is Structural Unemployment on the Rise?*, p.3.

[9] J. Bradford DeLong, "Is Today's Unemployment Structural?," *The Economists' Voice*, September 2010, http://www.bepress.com/ev.

[10] BLS, Local Area Unemployment Statistics (LAUS) program. LAUS data are available at http://stats.bls.gov/lau/.

[11] CRS calculations from state-by-state employment data available through BLS's Current Employment Statistics program at http://stats.bls.gov/sae/.

[12] See, for example, Regis Barnichon and Andrew Figura, *What Drives Matching Efficiency? A Tale of Composition and Dispersion*, Federal Reserve Board, Finance and Economics Discussion Series, No. 2011-10, January 9, 2011; Henry S. Farber, "Unemployment in the Great Recession: Did the Housing Market Crisis Prevent the Unemployed from Moving to Take Jobs?," *American Economics Review*, vol. 102, no. 3 (May 2012); Alicia Sasser Modestino and Julia Dennett, *Are American Homeowners Locked into Their Houses? The Impact of Housing Market Conditions on State-to-State Migration*, Federal Reserve Bank of Boston, Working Paper no. 12-1, February 8, 2012; and Sam Schulhofer-Wohl, *Negative Equity Does Not Reduce Homeowners' Mobility*, National Bureau of Economic Research, Working Paper no. 16701, January 2011.

[13] Raven Molloy, Christopher L. Smith, and Abigail Wozniak, "Internal Migration in the United States," *Journal of Economic Perspectives*, vol. 25, no. 3 (Summer 2011), pp. 173-196.

[14] Greg Kaplan and Sam Schulhofer-Wohl, *Interstate Migration Has Fallen Less Than You Think: Consequences of Hot Deck Imputation in the Current Population Survey*, Federal Reserve Bank of Minneapolis Working Paper 681, November 2010.

[15] Daniel Aaronson and Jonathan Davis, "How Much Has House Lock Affected Labor Mobility and the Unemployment Rate?," *Chicago Fed Letter*, no. 290, September 2011.

[16] The authors used BLS's definition of displaced workers, namely, those aged 20 and older who lost their jobs after being on their employers' payrolls for at least three years prior to displacement.

[17] John Schmitt and Kris Warner, *Deconstructing Structural Unemployment*, Center for Economic and Policy Research, May 24, 2011.

[18] Robert G. Valletta, *House Lock and Structural Unemployment*, Federal Reserve Bank of San Francisco Working Paper no. 2012-25, revised November 2012.

[19] Fatih Karahan and Serena Rhee, *Geographical Reallocation and Unemployment during the Great Recession: the Role of the Housing Bust*, University of Pennsylvania, 2011, available at http://economics JMP_Karahan.pdf.

[20] BLS defines a part-time work schedule as less than 35 hours a week.

[21] CRS calculations from Current Population Survey (CPS) data available at http://stats.bls.gov/cps/.

[22] Arjun Jayadev and Mike Konczal, *The Stagnating Labor Market*, The Roosevelt Institute, September 19, 2010, p. 8.

[23] BLS, Job Openings and Labor Turnover Survey (JOLTS) data are available at http://stats.bls.gov/jlt/.

[24] Infrastructure spending included in the American Recovery and Reinvestment Act of 2009 may have given a boost to hiring in the heavy and civil engineering component of the construction industry (i.e., establishments whose primary activity is the construction of entire engineering projects, such as highways, and specialty trade contractors whose primary activity is the production of a specific component for such projects). The law's provisions to encourage energy conservation among homeowners also may have contributed to increased labor demand in 2010 in the specialty trade contractors component of the construction industry (e.g., firms that install prefabricated thermal-pane window units and energy-efficient heating/air-conditioning units).

[25] The hiring rate of the federal government surpassed its pre-recession level in part because the Census Bureau hired temporary workers to help conduct the 2010 decennial census. For additional information, see BLS, *Census 2010 Temporary Workers and Intermittent Workers and Federal Government Employment,* available at http://stats.bls.gov/ces/cescensusworkers.pdf; and *Impact of 2010 Census Operations on Jobs and Economic Growth*, available at http://www.esa.doc.gov/sites/default/files/reports/documents/economic growth.pdf.

[26] For additional information, see CRS Report RL32292, *Offshoring (or Offshore Outsourcing) and Job Loss Among U.S. Workers*, by Linda Levine.

[27] The distribution of employment by occupation within industries is from BLS's Occupational Employment Survey, which is available at http://stats.bls.gov/oes/.

[28] The West is composed of Alaska, Arizona, California, Colorado, Hawaii, Idaho, Montana, Nevada, New Mexico, Oregon, Utah, Washington, and Wyoming. The South is composed of Alabama, Arkansas, Delaware, District of Columbia, Florida, Georgia, Kentucky,

Louisiana, Maryland, Mississippi, North Carolina, Oklahoma, South Carolina, Tennessee, Texas, Virginia, and West Virginia.

[29] The Midwest is composed of Illinois, Indiana, Iowa, Kansas, Michigan, Minnesota, Missouri, Nebraska, North Dakota, Ohio, South Dakota, and Wisconsin.

[30] The Northeast is composed of Connecticut, Maine, Massachusetts, New Hampshire, New Jersey, New York, Pennsylvania, Rhode Island, and Vermont.

[31] CRS calculations from CPS and JOLTS data.

[32] In late 2012, there were about three jobless workers per opening.

[33] The CPS data on unemployment by industry cover persons previously employed in a given industry, which suggests that by-and-large they possessed the skills needed to qualify for the jobs they lost or left. The CPS data on unemployment discussed in the initial paragraph of this section cover all unemployed persons, that is, new entrants and reentrants to the labor force as well as persons who lost or left their jobs.

[34] Aysegul Sahin, Joseph Song, Giorgio Topa and Giovanni L. Violante, *Mismatch Unemployment*, September 2012, p. 20. It is a revised version of *Mismatch Unemployment,* National Bureau of Economic Research, Working Paper no. 18265, August 2012. (Hereinafter referred to as Sahin et al., *Mismatch Unemployment.*)

[35] See for example John Silvia and Anika Khan, "Our Two Cents on Structural Unemployment," *ABA Banking Journal*, November 2010.

[36] Kathryn J. Byun ("The U.S. Housing Bubble and Bust: Impacts on Employment," *Monthly Labor Review*, December 2010) estimated that bubble-related demand accounted for between 1.2 million and 1.7 million residential-constructionrelated jobs in 2005 at the housing bubble's peak.

[37] For additional information, see CRS Report RS22915, *Temporary Extension of Unemployment Benefits: Emergency Unemployment Compensation (EUC08)*, by Katelin P. Isaacs and Julie M. Whittaker.

[38] Testimony of Lawrence F. Katz, Harvard University, on "Long-Term Unemployment in the Great Recession," in U.S. Congress, Joint Economic Committee, *Long-Term Unemployment: Causes, Consequences and Solutions*, 111th Cong., 2nd sess., April 29, 2010.

[39] Calculated by CRS from CPS data.

[40] There was also a brief recession in 1980.

[41] Some have speculated that other displaced workers, such as those formerly employed in the finance, insurance and real estate industries, may more easily find new jobs because their skills are more readily transferable to other industries than those of construction and manufacturing workers. See for example Ellen R. Rissman, "Employment Growth: Cyclical Movements or Structural Change?," *Federal Reserve Bank of Chicago Economic Perspectives*, 4th quarter 2009, pp. 40-57.

[42] After the 1981-1982 recession, the long-term unemployed's share of total unemployment grew to 23.9%. Their share next peaked in 2003, at 22.1%, during the recovery from the 2001 recession.

[43] For additional information, see CRS Report R41179, *Long-Term Unemployment and Recessions*, by Gerald Mayer and Linda Levine.

[44] Robert Shimer, "The Probability of Finding a Job," *American Economic Review*, vol. 98, no. 2 (May 2008), pp. 268- 273.

[45] Catherine Rampell, *Will Today's Unemployed Become Tomorrow's Unemployable?*, December 2, 2010, available at http://economix.blogs.

[46] Edward P. Lazear and James R. Spletzer, *The United States Labor Market: Status Quo or A New Normal?*, Paper presented at the Jackson Hole symposium, July 22, 2012, p. 32.

[47] Mark deWolf and Katherine Klemmer, "Job Openings, Hires, and Separations Fall During the Recession," *Monthly Labor Review*, May 2010, pp. 36-44.

[48] Regis Barnichon et al., "Which Industries are Shifting the Beveridge Curve?," *Monthly Labor Review*, June 2012.

[49] Mary Daly, Bart Hobijn, and Aysegul Sahin, et al.,"A Search and Matching Approach to Labor Markets: Did the Natural Rate of Unemployment Rise?," *Journal of Economic Perspectives*, vol. 26, no. 3 (summer 2012), p. 20.

[50] Sahin et al., *Mismatch Unemployment*.

[51] Benedikt Herz and Thijs van Rens, *Structural Unemployment*, Barcelona Graduate School of Economics, Working Paper no. 568, July 2011, available at http://www.crei.cat/~vanrens /SU/HvR_SU_201107.pdf.

[52] The increase in the duration of benefit eligibility to a 99-week maximum may have raised the unemployment rate above what it otherwise would have been by either reducing the number of long-term unemployed exiting the labor force or by reducing their intensity of job search and thereby decreasing the likelihood of reemployment, or both. For information on the relationship between unemployment duration and benefit receipt, see CRS Report R41676, *The Effect of Unemployment Insurance on the Economy and the Labor Market*, by Thomas L. Hungerford.

[53] Robert G. Valletta and Katherine Kuang, *Extended Unemployment and UI Benefits*, FRBSF Economic Letter, No. 2010-12, April 19, 2010.

[54] Jesse Rothstein, *Unemployment Insurance and Job Search in the Great Recession*, National Bureau of Economic Research, Working Paper no. 17534, October 2011.

[55] Daniel Aaronson, Bhashkar Mazumder, and Shani Schechter, "What is Behind the Rise in Long-Term Unemployment?," *Federal Reserve Bank of Chicago Economic Perspectives*, 2nd quarter 2010; and Bhashkar Mazumder, "How Did Unemployment Insurance Extensions Affect the Unemployment Rate in 2008-10?," *Chicago Fed Letter*, No. 285, April 2011.

[56] Shigeru Fujita, *Effects of Extended Unemployment Insurance Benefits: Evidence from the Monthly CPS*, Federal Reserve Bank of Philadelphia, Working Paper no. 10-35/R, January 2011; Steven D. Mullins, "The Unemployment Impact of the 2008 Extension of Unemployment Insurance: As High as Robert Barro Suggested?," *Economic Journal Watch*, vol. 9, no. 1, January 2012; and Makoto Nakajima, *A Quantitative Analysis of Unemployment Benefit Extension,*, Federal Reserve Bank of Philadelphia, Working Paper no. 11-8, February 8, 2011.

[57] For a discussion of institutional and other factors estimated to have led to inter-country differences in structural unemployment, see *Structural Unemployment in Western Europe*, ed. Martin Werding (Cambridge, MA: MIT Press, 2006).

[58] Michael W. Elsby, Bart Hobijn, and Aysegul Sahin, *The Labor Market in the Great Recession*, National Bureau of Economic Research, Working Paper no. 15979, May 2010. For the Brookings Panel on Economic Activity in September 2011, they along with Robert G. Valletta prepared *The Labor Market in the Great Recession: An Update,* dated October 2011, which was released by the Tinbergen Institute as Discussion Paper 2011-173/3.

[59] Structural unemployment rates vary across countries depending in part on differences in their labor market institutions or settings. The U.S. labor market is considered to be less rigid (more flexible) than that of many European countries partly because it's much lower unionization rate allows wages to adjust more quickly to economic shocks. Similarly, the relatively less generous unemployment insurance programs and lower public spending on active labor market programs (e.g., retraining) in the United States create smaller disincentives to job search among U.S. compared with European workers. See, for example,

Sven Jari Stehn, "Only a Modest Rise in Structural Unemployment So Far," *US Economics Analyst Issue No.: 10/34*, Goldman Sachs Global ECS US Research, August 27, 2010.

[60] Nicoletta Batini et al., *United States: Selected Issues Paper*, International Monetary Fund, Country Report No. 10/248, Washington, DC, July 2010, available at http://www.imf.org/external/pubs/ft/scr/2010/cr10248.pdf.

[61] Mary Daly, Bart Hobijn, and Rob Valletta, *The Recent Evolution of the Natural Rate of Unemployment*, FRBSF, Working Paper no. 2011-05, January 2011, p. 21.

[62] Stephanie Guichard and Elena Rusticelli, *Assessing the Impact of the Financial Crisis on Structural Unemployment in OECD Countries*, OECD, Economic Department Working Paper no. 767, Paris, France, October 14, 2010.

INDEX

#

2001 recession, 65, 68, 97, 99, 106

A

ABA, 106
access, 8, 42, 48
accessibility, 51
accommodation(s), 93, 95
accounting, 16, 33, 100
adjustment, 52, 71
adults, 6, 17, 38, 69, 81
African-American, 55
age, vii, viii, 2, 3, 4, 5, 8, 9, 12, 14, 15, 16, 17, 18, 20, 26, 40, 43, 45, 49, 52, 62, 69, 70, 71, 73, 79, 81
aggregate demand, xi, 50, 75, 86, 87, 89, 90, 93, 102
aging population, 8, 9, 12, 15, 48
Alaska, 91, 105
American Recovery and Reinvestment Act, 87, 104, 105
American Recovery and Reinvestment Act of 2009, 105
assessment, 63, 69, 92
attachment, 50
attitudes, 45
audit, 45
authority, 51

B

baby boomers, vii, viii, 1, 2, 6, 9, 14, 15, 45, 69
balanced budget, 76
beneficiaries, 32, 33
benefits, vii, 1, 9, 32, 39, 43, 45, 48, 50, 52, 72, 75, 76, 80, 88, 103
birth control, 40
birth rate, 13
blogs, 106
Britain, 55
Budget Committee, 104
budget deficit, ix, 48, 62, 76, 82
Bureau of Labor Statistics, 16, 56, 66, 68, 73
business cycle, vii, viii, x, 1, 2, 4, 9, 10, 20, 23, 26, 44, 52, 74, 76, 81, 85, 87, 88, 89, 98, 100
businesses, 50, 51

C

calculus, 36
caregivers, 88
causality, 79
Census, 92, 105
challenges, vii, 1, 5, 20, 47, 48
Chicago, 54, 105, 106, 107
childcare, 49

childrearing, 12
children, 6, 12, 13, 49
City, 59, 79
clarity, 51
colleges, 50
color, 49
community(s), 50, 95
competition, 38, 43
complementarity, 39
composition, x, 86, 88, 99
computer, 51
computing, 16
conditioning, 105
conference, 77, 80, 81, 82
Congress, ix, x, 51, 61, 62, 76, 82, 85, 86, 87, 99, 104, 106
Congressional Budget Office, 11, 48, 56, 64, 79, 80, 81, 82
consensus, viii, 61, 64, 75, 76
construction, 90, 93, 97, 99, 100, 105, 106
contraceptives, 8
correlation, 79, 80
covering, 74
credentials, 50
crises, 69
criticism, 80
curricula, 50
customers, 95
cycles, 19, 78
cyclical component, 10, 20, 21, 23, 34, 52, 64
cyclical unemployment, x, 85, 86, 87, 89, 90

D

danger, 47
data collection, 8
decomposition, 4, 23, 33, 71
deficit, 76, 82
deflationary pressures, 77
demographic change, viii, 2
demographic data, 71
demographic factors, 18
demographic inflection point, vii, 1
Department of Labor, 56
depth, ix, 62, 74, 75, 78, 100
deterrence, 45
developed countries, 40
direct measure, 11
disability, 27, 29, 31, 33, 69, 70, 71, 72, 80
discrimination, 8, 40, 51
dispersion, 90
displacement, 89, 105
distribution, viii, 2, 14, 16, 70, 71, 105
District of Columbia, 91, 105
divergence, 63
dream, 77

E

early retirement, vii, 1, 70, 72
earnings, 42, 43
economic activity, 50, 78, 87
economic conditions, viii, 2
economic crisis, vii, 1
economic growth, ix, 48, 49, 69, 85, 89, 105
economic indicator, ix, 62
Economic output, ix, 62
economic theory, x, 64, 74, 86, 87
economics, 81, 105
economists, ix, 36, 62, 64, 65, 74, 75, 76, 78, 79, 82, 86, 100, 101
education, x, 8, 19, 38, 44, 45, 50, 73, 86
education/training, 73
educational attainment, 19, 27, 70
educational services, 93
empirical studies, 39, 89, 101
employees, 40, 48, 88, 93, 95, 99
employers, x, 45, 48, 50, 51, 52, 66, 75, 86, 89, 90, 97, 98, 100, 105
employment, viii, ix, x, 6, 9, 36, 38, 44, 45, 48, 50, 61, 62, 63, 65, 66, 72, 73, 74, 76, 77, 78, 79, 80, 82, 83, 86, 87, 90, 91, 95, 96, 97, 104, 105
employment growth, 65, 76, 80, 90
employment opportunities, 44, 50, 74
energy, 105
energy conservation, 105
engineering, 105
enrollment, viii, 4, 11, 34, 35, 36, 62

equity, 76
erosion, 83
Europe, 75
evidence, ix, 5, 10, 11, 32, 38, 62, 70, 75, 77, 80, 90, 92
evolution, vii, viii, 2, 45, 47
exercise, 87

F

families, vii, 1, 13, 42, 49
family life, 45
fast food, 95
federal funds, 77, 82
federal government, 95, 105
Federal Housing Finance Agency (FHFA), 51
Federal Reserve, x, 11, 55, 56, 57, 59, 64, 79, 80, 81, 82, 85, 87, 102, 104, 105, 106, 107
Federal Reserve Board, 59, 102, 104
fertility, 19
fillers, 95
financial, 69, 74, 77, 87, 93, 103
financial crisis, 74, 77, 87, 93, 103
fiscal policy, ix, x, 48, 62, 76, 82, 85
fitness, 95
flexibility, 48
fluctuations, 89, 98, 102
food, 93, 95
food services, 93, 95
force, vii, viii, 1, 2, 3, 5, 6, 8, 12, 14, 19, 23, 33, 34, 35, 38, 39, 40, 44, 45, 48, 49, 50, 51, 61, 63, 66, 67, 68, 70, 72, 73, 79, 80, 81, 88, 89, 99
foreclosure, 51
foreign investment, 51
formal education, 87
foundations, 50
France, 108
frictional unemployment, 88
full employment, viii, ix, 18, 46, 47, 50, 61, 62, 63, 64, 65, 74, 75, 76, 77, 78, 79, 82
funding, 50
funds, 50, 52, 77

G

GDP, 6, 11, 48, 82
Georgia, 105
goods and services, x, 85, 87, 88
Great Depression, viii, 61, 63
Great Recession, vii, viii, ix, 1, 2, 3, 4, 5, 6, 9, 10, 11, 19, 20, 23, 26, 33, 40, 46, 51, 56, 58, 59, 62, 63, 65, 68, 69, 73, 74, 75, 78, 79, 80, 81, 82, 83, 100, 102, 104, 105, 106, 107
growth, x, 5, 6, 11, 43, 46, 50, 65, 66, 69, 76, 79, 86, 87, 104
growth rate, 6
guidance, 77

H

Hawaii, 105
health, 38, 39, 48, 67, 69, 93, 98
health care, 93
health insurance, 48
health services, 98
high school, 34, 44, 45, 50
high school degree, 44
higher education, 49
highways, 105
hiring, 5, 27, 45, 51, 89, 95, 96, 105
history, vii, 1
homeowners, 51, 91, 92, 105
homes, 92, 97
hospitality, 98
House, 105
housing, 51, 69, 91, 92, 93, 95, 97, 101, 106
housing bust, 93
human, 18
human capital, 18
hypothesis, 22, 25, 27, 45, 69, 92
hysteresis, 74, 75, 78, 81, 83

I

imbalances, 90
IMF, 82, 102

immigrants, 48
immigration, 5, 48
improvements, 38, 39
incarceration, 45
incidence, 98
income, 35, 38, 49, 88
income tax, 88
increased competition, 38
individuals, 3, 5, 12, 14, 16, 18, 26, 47, 48, 49, 73, 80
industry(s), x, 27, 32, 43, 50, 51, 86, 87, 89, 90, 93, 95, 97, 98, 99, 100, 105, 106
inflation, ix, 62, 64, 75, 76, 77, 78, 79, 83, 87, 89, 102
inflection points, vii, 2
infrastructure, 50, 51
injury, 69
institutions, x, 86, 88, 107
interest rates, ix, 62, 77
Internal Revenue Service, 92
International Monetary Fund, 79, 80, 81, 82, 102, 108
international trade, 40, 43
investment(s), 50
Iowa, 106
issues, 4, 51

J

Japan, 42, 55
job availability, viii, 2
job creation, 87
job matching, 88
job training, 50
job training programs, 50
job-finding prospects, viii, 2
jobless, x, 74, 86, 88, 89, 99, 100, 106
joblessness, x, 86
jobseekers, x, 86, 97
Joint Economic Committee, 106

L

labor force participation, vii, viii, 2, 3, 5, 6, 8, 11, 12, 14, 16, 19, 20, 23, 26, 34, 35, 38, 39, 40, 42, 43, 44, 45, 48, 49, 50, 52, 61, 63, 67, 68, 69, 73, 76, 79, 80, 81
labor market(s), viii, ix, x, 23, 45, 47, 50, 61, 62, 63, 65, 72, 75, 76, 77, 78, 86, 88, 89, 92, 93, 94, 95, 99, 100, 103, 107
labor shortage, 90
laws, 40
layoffs, x, 86, 99
legislation, 8
leisure, 39
leisure time, 39
life cycle, 12
life expectancy, 12, 18, 19, 38
lifetime, 12
linear model, 52
logging, 98
longevity, 8, 9, 39, 46
Louisiana, 106

M

macroeconomic policy(s), 75, 78
magnitude, 15, 88
majority, 4, 9, 10, 16, 89
manufacturing, 51, 90, 106
marriage, 19
married women, 42
Maryland, 106
media, 79, 81
median, 9
medical, 48
Medicare, 48
metropolitan areas, 92
Mexico, 105
microeconomic policies, 63
migration, 91, 92, 93
minimum wage(s), 19
Minneapolis, 102, 105
Missouri, 106

monetary policy(s), ix, x, 62, 63, 76, 77, 85, 87
Montana, 105

N

natural rate of unemployment, 64, 65, 74, 75, 76, 78, 81, 89
negative effects, 43
negative relation, 38, 101
nonmarket activities, 6
normal aging, 47
Norway, 42

O

Obama, 5
Obama Administration, 5
obstacles, 88
OECD, 103, 108
Office of Management and Budget, 64
offshoring, 95
Oklahoma, 106
output gap, 76, 82
outreach, 52
outsourcing, 95
oversight, 76

P

pain, vii, 1
parents, 49
payroll, 66
peace, 13
Philadelphia, 57, 107
plausibility, 27
playing, vii, 2
polarization, 36, 38
policy, ix, x, 4, 5, 39, 46, 47, 48, 49, 62, 63, 72, 76, 77, 78, 80, 86, 89
policy choice, 47
policy makers, 63, 72, 76, 78
policymakers, ix, 85, 88
population, vii, 2, 3, 4, 5, 9, 12, 14, 15, 16, 17, 20, 26, 34, 38, 45, 65, 66, 67, 69, 70, 82
positive relationship, 101
potential output, 69, 82, 83
preparation, 95
present value, 52
president, 1, 11, 47, 48, 49, 50, 51, 64, 74, 102
President Obama, 51
price index, 92
price stability, 76, 78
primacy, 95
private sector, 51
probability, 92, 100
product market, 103
productivity growth, 6, 104
prosperity, 13

Q

questionnaire, 70, 71

R

real estate, 95, 106
reality, 76
reasoning, 23
recall, 89
recession, viii, ix, x, 3, 6, 11, 16, 17, 20, 27, 32, 34, 38, 43, 61, 62, 63, 64, 65, 68, 69, 70, 72, 73, 75, 76, 78, 80, 82, 85, 86, 87, 89, 90, 92, 93, 95, 96, 97, 98, 99, 100, 101, 105, 106
recovery, vii, viii, ix, x, 1, 4, 5, 6, 17, 26, 32, 34, 45, 50, 51, 52, 61, 63, 64, 65, 67, 69, 72, 73, 74, 75, 76, 78, 80, 85, 86, 87, 92, 95, 97, 98, 99, 100, 106
recreation, 93, 95
recruiting, 51, 98
reform(s), 5, 40, 43, 48, 82
regression, 21, 22, 23, 25, 27, 33, 34, 52
regulations, 103
repair, 95

replacement rate, 88
requirements, x, 86, 88, 89
researchers, 4, 11, 51, 103
resources, 64
response, 20, 48, 78, 87, 93
restrictions, 23
retail, 93, 95, 98
retirement, vii, viii, ix, 1, 2, 6, 8, 9, 14, 17, 18, 39, 40, 46, 62, 63, 69, 71, 72, 78, 80, 88
retirement age, 14, 39, 80
revenue, 76
risk(s), 51, 78
rules, 49

S

savings, 18
school, viii, 5, 11, 19, 27, 33, 34, 35, 36, 49, 62, 69, 71, 72, 81
school enrollment, 19, 27, 33, 35, 36, 69, 71, 72
schooling, 6, 12, 29, 31, 34, 36, 38, 71
scope, 63, 82
security, 50
self-employed, 39, 48, 66
self-employment, 48
seminars, 80, 81, 82
Senate, 48, 104
services, 98
shape, 6
shock, 6, 19
shortfall, 100
showing, 9
significance level, 23
signs, 80, 99
social norms, 8
Social Security, vii, 1, 9, 11, 14, 19, 32, 38, 39, 43, 45, 48, 55, 57, 58, 80, 88
Social Security Administration, 14, 80
Social Security Disability Insurance, 11, 32
society, viii, 2, 8, 88
South Dakota, 106
specifications, 21, 23, 34
speculation, 91
speech, 81, 102
spending, 63, 76, 78, 105, 107
Spring, 55
stability, 78
stabilization, ix, 62, 63, 76, 82
standard error, 22, 24, 29, 31
state(s), viii, 5, 20, 38, 61, 63, 70, 74, 75, 77, 80, 90, 91, 92, 93, 95, 101, 102, 104
statistics, 17
stigma, 75
stimulus, x, 76, 77, 78, 83, 86, 87
stock, 95
structural changes, ix, 5, 62, 63, 78
structural unemployment, x, 86, 87, 88, 89, 90, 97, 99, 101, 102, 103, 107
structure, x, 14, 18, 23, 45, 86
subgroups, 34

T

target, 49, 77
Task Force, 50
technological change, 43
technology, 8, 39, 40, 43
teens, 36, 38
tellers, 95
testing, 26
time periods, 9, 10
time series, 10, 11, 17, 20, 21, 23, 33, 52
Title I, 8, 40
Title V, 8, 40
trade, 93, 95, 97, 98, 105
training, viii, 50, 52, 62, 69, 87
traits, 27
trajectory, 6, 48
transportation, 50

U

U.S. Bureau of Labor Statistics, 91, 94, 96, 104
U.S. economy, vii, 1, 103
U.S. labor market, ix, 62, 99, 107
U.S. Social Security Administration, 80

unemployed individuals, 5
unemployment insurance, 75, 107
unemployment rate, viii, ix, x, xi, 3, 11, 20, 23, 26, 33, 61, 62, 63, 64, 65, 66, 72, 73, 74, 75, 76, 77, 78, 79, 80, 81, 82, 85, 86, 87, 89, 90, 93, 97, 98, 99, 100, 101, 102, 103, 107
United, 6, 40, 42, 55, 75, 80, 81, 82, 95, 99, 102, 103, 105, 106, 107, 108
United Kingdom, 42
United States, 6, 40, 42, 55, 75, 80, 81, 82, 95, 99, 102, 103, 105, 106, 107, 108
updating, 103
Urban Institute, 57, 58, 59

V

vacancies, 75, 97, 98, 100
variables, 19, 29, 31
variations, 75, 103
volatility, 6
vulnerability, 103

W

wage structure, 43, 57
wages, 43, 76, 90, 107
war, 13, 69
Washington, 57, 58, 59, 105, 108
weakness, 72
wealth, 19, 40, 69
Western Europe, 107
White House, 49
Wisconsin, 106
work-center, 40
workforce, 5, 11, 12, 42, 43
working families, 49
workplace, 5, 39, 48, 50
World War I, viii, 13, 61, 65, 67, 68

Y

young adults, 49
young people, 35, 36, 50
young women, 42
youth unemployment, ix, 62, 73